MEMPHIS TYPE HISTORY

Signs and Stories From Just Around the Corner

CAITLIN L. HORTON

Artwork by Rebecca Phillips

This book is, of course, dedicated to Memphis.
We hope we've told these few stories of yours well.

Contents

Preface

Jeremy Greene and I have not worked on many projects together but we did work in the same building; and he was someone I looked up to for creative and freelance advice. He is an amazing videographer, photographer, and overall craftsman; so when he mentioned he would be working on a personal summer project in 2010 called Memphis Type – a project in which he would be photographing intriguing signs, graffiti, and typography throughout the city – I waited in anticipation. I have had great fondness for typography and hand-painted signs for many years, but in no way do I have the photographic skills to reproduce these land treasures the way Mr. Greene does. Through his talented lens, sometimes equipped with just his iPhone, Jeremy spotted and captured the character of many signs throughout the city. I waited every week for the new Memphis Type photograph and any moment I came across one of these landmarks on the street, a small rush of joyous satisfaction overcame me as though I had found "Where's Waldo" in Memphis. I had lived in Memphis for just a couple of years at that time, so it was through Memphis Type that I was introduced to signs like Leahy's, Skateland, Universal Life Co., and so many others. Through Memphis Type, Jeremy unintentionally introduced me to another beautiful characteristic of this city I grew to love so well - historic and detailed signage. As I watched the collection of photographs grow, I wanted to paint them, to create another form of documentation, another art form of this craft. Jeremy graciously allowed me to paint

replications of his photographs, and so began the series I called Memphis Type Illustrated.

Memphis Type Illustrated consisted of eleven 18" by 18" acrylic on hardboard paintings, all composed in the studio space of Jeremy's old office. I believe I intended to gain some knowledge of photography as a side benefit to being in that studio, yet I mostly discovered how much I missed and loved painting, and, since I was in near proximity for Jeremy to compare his photographs to my paintings, I held my breath expecting some sort of disapproval. Instead, I had the privilege to hear his past stories, like his anxiety teaching himself how to edit video before beginning his first professional job as a video editor and his living in a mansion with his family for free during summers. Surprisingly, the stories were another reason why I fell in love with painting landmarks. When I displayed the series at an art show in Downtown Memphis, a woman came to me and said she lived at Leahy's for over 30 years and had some of the best memories of her life there. Her story was the first but certainly not the last.

I never would have dreamed or expected an opportunity to seek out and collect the historical stories behind these fascinating landmarks. Nevertheless, Caitlin Horton, who I met a couple of years later, was on a mission to begin a new online gallery in which she would not only market and sell artwork, but also tell the stories behind artists and their work. With her extraordinary help, the Memphis Type Illustrated series reached out to a broader audience. The History Press provided the way to document these landmarks at another level, and, in so doing, bestowed upon me the greatest little adventure. Caitlin assembled a little blog for us to collect stories and information called Memphis Type History which allowed people to see who we are and what we are about. Naturally, through research and collecting stories I have fallen even more in love with each landmark. I have had the honor to sit across the table from June West, Executive Director of Memphis Heritage – a woman I call my Memphis hero – and listen to the process of how Overton Square was spared from becoming a single grocery store. I sat in Jimmy Ogle's car and listened to his outstandingly abundant knowledge of Memphis history as we drove around different areas of downtown. I was offered a drink and cotton candy at the Skateland Raleigh concession stand as I listened to the rink's charming family history. I cried when I heard Willie Earl Bates speak of Soulsville and what his love for and contribution from that community means to him. I have shared tears, laughter, and surprises with people who's stories unfold and remind me why this city is so incredible and so endearing. To express how thankful and blessed I feel to have partaken in this journey is rather quite difficult because I assure you it has been great.

Sincerely,
Rebecca L. Phillips

One of Jeremy Greene's early Memphis Type photographs.

Acknowledgements

From Caitlin: My first thanks must go to my husband, Kennedy, whose love and support has allowed me to say yes to the unexpected opportunities that have come my way. He is a source of ideas, a sounding board, a voice of reason, and just all around the best partner in life a girl could ever hope for. Special thanks goes to Rebecca, who invited me to join her in creating this book. I'm so glad you allowed me to go along for the ride.

To my parents and brother, thank you for being such a great family and enthusiastic support system. A bit of extra appreciation goes to Mom and Dad for teaching me to love reading and writing. So far that's come in really handy. Also, another thank you to my dad – without all those convoluted stories you told us, I wouldn't have known how to wait for the gems in people's stories, even when it's sometimes a long and winding road to get there.

To my grandparents, thank you for always being so interested in the unusual things your grandkids are doing. I have no doubt that the Jumbo stories out on the swing and the rabbit stories at bedtime helped me tell the stories of these Memphis landmarks. To my other grandparents who have gone on ahead: Although you are not here, it is a gift to know how proud you are of me because you always were when you were with us.

A big thanks goes out to all my in-laws. The Hortons, Buckners, Cummins, and Harts have all been enthusiastic cheerleaders throughout this whole project. I'm so thankful to be a part of such a great family.

Finally, I must acknowledge and thank God for putting all these people in my life who made it possible for me to be here today. I don't know what's coming next but I do know You are already there.

From Rebecca: I'd like to thank my mother for always telling a good story, for giving birth to me, and for raising children which I now realize are two difficult things to do in life. While growing up, her superstitions and traditions kept life interesting. Thanks to my sister, Melissa, for always telling a good joke and helping me find the lighter side of things. She's the best and most unusual sister I could have ever asked for. Thanks to my father, the best craftsman I know, who inspired me to draw and taught me to pay attention to detail. Those old car models and wood projects were fun to work on. I'd like to thank my daughter, Edie, even though she's merely a toddler and hardly speaks full sentences, she certainly is an incredible joy in my life. Thanks to my husband, Michael, who has been the most supportive person in my life since the day he offered me guitar lessons. He understands my humor, my flaws, my fears, and we go together.

In other news, this project and inspiration would not be possible without Jeremy Greene. I am thankful for his creative advice and encouragement, his attempt to teach me about photography, though ultimately he taught me more about Memphis in general.

I'd like to thank Hazard, Kentucky. Oddly, after only living there two years, I will never forget the people and mountains. It was a charming and culturally different experience but a place that welcomed us so graciously and ultimately led us to Memphis.

On a grand level, I thank God. I have faith He is the creator and supplied me with a skill and love to paint. I am also grateful He is always near.

Thanks to Grandma Weaver for the fur hat. She was a classy lady and I hope to be like her.

From Both of Us: Together we must thank the good folks of Memphis who told us so many wonderful stories. Without their memories and a willingness to share them with us, this book would not have been possible. Big thanks go out to master tour guide, Jimmy Ogle, who gave us a whirlwind driving tour of Downtown in the pouring rain that we will never forget. Thanks to the other wonderful people who gave us tours and extensive information about their industries. They helped us understand so much more about sign making, rubber stamps, music, roller skating, education, and more.

We will always treasure the small business owners who gave us their time and told us whatever they could about these unusual signs we asked so many questions about. Among those is Jimmie Tucker, who brought us into the Universal Life Insurance Company building and painted a picture of its future. Words can't express how appreciative we are of our time with Mr. Willie Bates, who shared his heart for the Soulsville community with us and fed us the South's finest turkey and dressing.

We may never personally meet others who helped us so generously. A huge thanks goes to Debra Jane Seltzer, who so willingly shared about her time spent with an obscure sign inventor the world never really forgot, and gave us access to the wealth of information she collected over the years. Thanks to Michael Gestring and Bill Goodwin who allowed us access to their wonderful Summer Avenue Gang Facebook group. Many stories in this book came from members of that group, who willingly and happily shared their memories about Memphis with us. We appreciate the kind people who worked hard to preserve Memphis history in the Shelby County Collections room at the Benjamin L. Hooks Central Library and in Special Collections at the University of Mississippi.

We appreciate the addition of Delonda Anderson to our team. She served as our editor, and really polished everything up. We certainly thank her for it.

Finally, to anyone who feels we might have inadvertently forgotten you on this list, we're thanking you right now too.

Introduction

The nature of signs is to represent something greater than themselves. In this book you will find that signs are the gateway for the stories of the businesses and the people who lived, worked, and sometimes sought safe haven, behind them. Examples like the Universal Life Insurance Company, during the time of Dr. Martin Luther King, Jr.'s, assassination, or the Lorraine Motel for Stax recording artists, or even the great Sam Phillips, whose desire for creative change started Sam Phillips Recording Studio. Each chapter offers a glimpse into various slices of life across time and geography. The people who interacted with what the signs symbolize are interesting and important both socially and historically.

One of the most recognizable signs in this book, the Sputnik at Joe's Liquors, represents the creative vision of a quiet inventor, hardly known to the world, who gifted us with spectacular road signs across the country. The Sputnik also represents how a community will rally around something it loves to restore it to a former glory. While interesting, the engineering specs of the Sputnik do not tell anything about the sign's true importance because a sign is a reflection of something more important than itself.

The history concerning most of these places is discovered exclusively in the stories people tell. The little slices of life, the people who accomplished so much in the businesses behind these logos, and the way these signs overlooked the city's transformation, combine to form a colorful history of Memphis. Therefore, the businesses' histories, as told by people who experienced them, tie the book together. Their stories reveal what life was like for people of all walks of life throughout several decades in Memphis.

Through hours of interviews and research, we discovered that each of these places experienced changes we can all relate to: political movements, technology, and customers' whims. The signs remained even after major changes in the surrounding area or in the evolution of the business the signs represented. In some cases, like Leahy's Weekly Rentals, the signs featured here are now gone. In others, like the Chicago Pizza Factory archway, they have been recreated to express something new without forgetting the old.

In the pages that follow, an intersection of art, history, and personal stories will allow an atmospheric experience of Memphis through paintings, photography, and personal stories. Passersby have whizzed by some of these signs for years without really taking a second glance. Others may already know quite a bit about these signs and their histories. Whatever the case, we hope you'll discover a little something new. Here, you will get a glimpse into what the places behind the signs once were and what they will become. By the time this book finds its way to some of you, it's likely some of these places will already be different from what we have described here. Our hope is that this book will encourage you to explore Memphis in a new way by rekindling your love for the unusual, the overlooked, and the hidden art before our eyes.

"UNIVERSAL LIFE WAS A HAVEN AND A REFUGE AND A PLACE THAT WAS ACTIVELY INVOLVED IN MAKING SURE THAT THE CIVIL RIGHTS MOVEMENT WENT FORWARD." — ART GILLIAM

Painting of Universal Life Insurance Company sign. **Rebecca Phillips**

THE UNIVERSAL LIFE INSURANCE COMPANY LEGACY

After celebrating their new office space at 480 Linden Avenue for two days, Universal Life Insurance Company employees got to work. The year was 1949, and their new Egyptian Revival style building represented more than just additional space for a growing company. "Designed by African-American-owned Nashville architecture firm McKissack & McKissack, at a cost of $450,000, it boasted thirty thousand square feet of work space with an employee cafeteria, an auditorium that sat 350 people, and the latest air conditioning technology," described the company's retrospective on the building in its 1973 annual review. Special cut stone from Russellville, Alabama enhanced the building's façade.

Memphis architect Jimmie Tucker looks back on the choice in architectural style with appreciation. "With this being an African-American owned insurance company, the leaders wanted to select a building style that had some connections to the founders and their typical customers. So they chose the Egyptian Revival style." The style was in keeping with the African-American community's interest in Egyptian history, culture, and art that developed around the 1920s. The design of the new building was in stark contrast to the company's former office space, a typical two-story downtown building. The new offices reflected the stature of the company with architecture that was uncommon in Memphis. "As I understand it, there's only about three buildings of that style in the city," reflects Tucker. John Hopkins of Memphis Heritage, Inc., praised the design of the company's new home office on Linden Avenue as, "the youngest example of Egyptian Revival architecture in the city, yet it is the most exuberant."

The venture began with Dr. Joseph Edison Walker, son of former slaves in Tillman, Mississippi. He completed medical school in Nashville, Tennessee, and practiced from 1909 to 1919 in Indianola, Mississippi. His medical education gained him early respect in the African-American community but his business endeavors forged Dr. Walker's greatest contributions. His business career began when he established one of the first African-American banks in Mississippi, the Delta Penny Savings Bank. He went on to help start the Mississippi Life Insurance Company. In 1923, Dr. Walker founded Universal Life Insurance Company (ULICO) in Memphis with Archie W. Willis and Mark Williams Bonner. Walker is also credited with founding the Memphis Negro Chamber of Commerce in 1926. In the forties, he opened Tri-State Bank with his son, Antonio Maceo Walker, which became a bastion of business in the African-American community. Under Dr. Walker's leadership, ULICO became the fourth largest African-American owned business in the U.S. by 1979. His son grew the firm from a 9.2 million dollar company to nearly 50 million dollars under his twenty-five years of management.

Not only was ULICO the fourth largest African-American owned insurance company in the U.S., the establishment was active in minority and civil rights issues. Shortly after

Universal Life Insurance Company interior, 1949. **Memphis and Shelby County Room, Memphis Public Library and Information Center.**

World War II, ULICO financed the Riverview Project, which was "the first large black housing subdivision in the entire South." Some four hundred houses helped move "many black people into decent homes for the first time." In 1950, the J.E. Walker subdivision was built, and boasted more than double the previous project's number of homes. Elliston Heights soon followed.

According to A. Maceo Walker, ULICO helped the NAACP get started in Memphis by providing them rent-free space for three years. In 1973, Reverend Jesse Jackson spoke at the company's fiftieth anniversary celebration. Jackson reiterated what Universal Life recognized many years before – that African

Americans must overcome the "economic roadblock." The company supported numerous nonprofits, gave to educational institutions, and provided scholarships for minorities. Most of all, Universal Life changed the perspective on black businesses and allowed many African Americans to achieve dreams they thought were unreachable.

Long-time ULICO employee J. T. Chandler started at the company when it was just five years old. As he recalled his time there in the fiftieth anniversary book, Chandler focused on the strong sense of accomplishment and identity the company afforded him, "One of the things I often thought of as a youngster was the opportunity of a life's career among my own people – a career in the black community with a black business. Today with most of my life behind me, I can say my entire life as an adult has been spent serving my own people as a member of all black-owned businesses." Chandler continued to address how companies like ULICO changed the landscape of opportunity for African Americans in that time, "...a generation or so ago most Negroes felt they must be employed by whites if they expected worthwhile lives of accomplishments; the education of their children and owning their homes. Fortunately, the Universal Life Insurance Company and other black-owned companies have gradually changed that opinion." The successes of his four children – all employed as Universal Life or Tri-State Bank public servants – was evidence of these facts. This kind of

legacy causes many to appreciate this landmark Memphis business to this day.

Others who saw their work at ULICO help advance their community echoed Chandler's sentiments. "In spite of the economic conditions of the black people and the many factors that made it difficult to build a progressive and solid life insurance company at that time, I was convinced that if we, as Negroes, were to become – by any means – an important factor in building any type of economic foundation for ourselves, it was of major importance that we build strong financial institutions," penned B. G. Olive, Jr., First Vice President-Secretary, in 1973. He recalled how difficult it was for ULICO to even get started. Very little training existed on how to run a life insurance company. What did exist was not made available to

The Universal Life Insurance Company building is a rare example of the Egyptian Revival style in Memphis. **Special Collections, University of Memphis Libraries.**

The interior of the ULICO building still features the original vinyl floor tiles and the original marble finish on the walls. **Jeremy Greene.**

African Americans. "In the black companies, we had to do a tremendous amount of research…" Olive explained, as he recounted the huge amount of study and strategy adjustments that went into starting the company. This experience was likely one that prompted the extensive, consistent, and ongoing training ULICO offered their employees.

Universal Life played a major role in the social and political life of the entire African-American community as its impact reached much further than the company's employees. "It was part of the fabric of the community. In fact, not only did Dr. Walker found both those institutions [Universal Life and Tri-State Bank], but also Mississippi Boulevard Mission Church. So Universal worked hand-in-hand with the church community as well as the civil rights community. The breadth of what they did went exponentially and enormously

beyond just the employee base," explains Art Gilliam. Gilliam also recalls an incident that occurred a few days before Dr. Martin Luther King, Jr., was slain, that captures how much the company meant to both himself and the black community, "There were riots that broke out and the police were attacking people who were just in establishments that were not necessarily involved with the protests. I happened to be in Universal Life Insurance looking out across what would be Danny Thomas [now]. There was a dining place called The Big M that was across from Universal Life Insurance. Police went in… and we saw them dragging people out and beating them. Several of those people who were beaten and were able to get away and weren't arrested actually came across the street and came into Universal Life as a refuge from that, from the activities that were taking place on the part of the police at that time." He

Rev. Dr. Benjamin Hooks

Remnants of the past, like this photo wall, recall the hundreds of employees who once worked here. Memphian and civil rights leader Benjamin L. Hooks' photo is at the center. **Jeremy Greene.**

explains, "That story, although it's about a very specific incident, tells the story of Universal Life Insurance in many ways because Universal Life was a haven and a refuge and a place that was actively involved in making sure that the civil rights movement went forward."

Universal Life saw nothing but success for decades. A 1966 *Commercial Appeal* article said, "The company represents a tower of strength in the local economy and the areas it serves... The officers of this young, but progressive company had dreamed of the day when one could look with pride at this institution of public service and have full confidence in the future of this monument to social, economic, financial and interracial progress and good will." Through hard work and dedication, the company grew tremendously in a competitive industry as it catered to a "thin market" of black customers.

Changes eventually came. By the 1980s, ULICO found itself competing more and more with all the other insurance companies on the market who now served both black and white communities. The ULICO model that provided "home service," or door-to-door collections, was in decline. Among other solutions, the company attempted to diversify its products, explored potentially lucrative joint ventures, and shifted its collection model from weekly to monthly, to no avail.

ULICO may have closed its doors, but this never affected its legacy. "The point is that, quiet though it has been kept, virtually every major advance made by blacks in this city is traceable directly or indirectly to Universal Life Insurance Co. and Tri-State Bank," wrote Gilliam in *The Commercial Appeal*. Willie Bates recalls

the lasting impression Gilliam made on him as his trainer at the Universal Life Insurance Company. Bates now owns The Four Way in the south Memphis neighborhood where he grew up. "I actually started my journey in the insurance business, right on this same corner [as The Four Way], with Universal Life Insurance," Bates says, remembering that 1961 summer. "I didn't have a car, but I'd ride the bus." He remembers how everyone there accepted him "on an equal basis," even if he came from less than they did. Bates began as an agent and continually moved up the ranks.

Bates carries on the legacy of his Universal Life role models. Now the owner of a historic Memphis restaurant, he plays a part in the Soulsville Foundation's revitalization efforts in his community. "I had a great experience at Universal. I don't think I would've been bold enough or prepared enough to take on the venture here at The Four Way except to have had the background, training, and nurturing of the Universal Life Insurance Company. Without that experience, perhaps somebody else would've been dealing with The Four Way. Maybe at worst The Four Way would've... disappeared or met with demolition, I don't know," he speculates, appreciating how the company made the life he's led possible.

Self+Tucker Architects acquired the building with the expectation it would become a turning point for the revitalization of the entire neighborhood. "The building, the history of the company, those people who were so important to making the company a success, they're among a group of important Memphians who are not widely known. So more broadly our goal is to make people aware of a lot of the history and evolution of our city," says Jimmie Tucker. He hopes to develop a way to tell the story so that it will inspire and capture the imagination of tourists and locals alike. "Part of what we're doing is research and highlighting the past. But it very much is about how we can make a better future for the area," he explains.

For Bates, the legacy of the Universal Life Insurance Company is all around him, from the pictures on his restaurant's walls to the church down the street, to the college right around the corner. The building is an important symbol of the people who made an impact on an entire city. "It is a jewel for this entire community... It's a bridge over times like these. Because there's still so much that we need to do and can do. So what better reflection could you have than a reflection of Universal Life in downtown Memphis, where so many people knew about the struggle and the benefits of it? It's an encouraging reference," he says.

Exterior of ULICO building and company sign, 2014. **Jeremy Greene.**

Painting of Advance Rubber Stamp Works sign. The sign remains mounted on the building at 339 Madison Avenue. **Rebecca Phillips.**

THE GHOSTS OF ADVANCE RUBBER STAMPS

The empty building at 339 Madison Avenue still wears reminders of its past, namely the large sign above the door. A giant hand holds an old-fashioned wooden stamp beside the words, Advance Rubber Stamps, all outlined in neon. Above the sign, three different families resided in the upstairs apartment, while their multiple businesses stayed busy underneath, in an industry that evolved and changed over the last century.

Blueprints for this property were drawn in May of 1913, and construction was completed just as the U.S. entered World War I, in April 1917. In its first life, the building housed the plumbing, electrical, and heating company Cronin, Baker & Tindall. "Memphis Greets You," a publication by the Business Men's Club – Chamber of Commerce, praised the company for its modern product line, applauded its unique business model, and admired their truly avant-garde showroom, with lighting and plumbing fixtures that dripped from the ceiling and glinted on every available tabletop. The publication noted, "The show rooms reflect the latest patterns in all that pertains to plumbing, bathroom fixtures and electrical furnishings. In fact, there is not a new thing on the market in that line that is not to be found there. The display of the wares and furnishings handled by the firm is proof of the fact that only the latest and most modern of equipment is handled." Undoubtedly some of these "latest patterns" were among those Cronin, Baker & Tindall installed in high-end locales like the Cotton Exchange and hotels like the Peabody, the Chisca, and the Gayoso.

Cronin, Baker & Tindall staff was described as "sober and painstaking." Perhaps these traits were due to the unusual structure of the business that made employees company stockholders. "This business policy has made their workmen more proficient than the average 'hired' force and has given a tone to their operations which places them in the front rank of artistic plumbers and electricians," said their profile in "Memphis Greets You."

In 1944, the Gruenbergs purchased the building from William Cronin's widow for $17,000. Three years later, the Gruenberg brothers Paul and William, and Lillian M. Gruenberg paid twenty dollars to file the corporate charter for Advance Rubber Stamp Works, Inc. The brothers renovated the building, adding both the Advance Rubber Stamps sign out front and an apartment upstairs, where the family lived.

One of the Gruenbergs' long-time employees was Thomas A. Davis. Davis began Accurate Engraving Service with his wife, Wylodine. The fledgling business operated out of their daughter's bedroom at first, then in 1978 they purchased the Madison Avenue building as well as the Gruenbergs' business. They ran Advance Rubber Stamp Works, Inc., and Accurate Engraving Service for the next 27 years.

The businesses changed hands to Charles and Regina Hodges in 2004. The Hodges changed the company names to Advance Rubber Stamp Works and Accurate Graphics. Under the Hodges' management, the business focused more on signage and printing than engraving small items. The fixtures and lighting showroom turned stamp company transformed into a building that housed two distinct businesses. "When you walked in, one side was Advance Rubber Stamps and one side was Accurate Graphics. Depending on what you needed you went to this person or that person," recalls Jeremy Smith, co-owner of Sign Smiths.

In 2012, Jeremy and Christopher Smith purchased both of Hodges' businesses and formed Sign Smiths. They operated from the Madison Avenue building for the first year. Jeremy Smith not only worked in the building, but when the day was done he walked upstairs to the apartment where he lived until Sign Smiths relocated in 2013. The year spent there with his two children marked the third time owners of the building called it home. The hundred-year-old building made an impression on Smith. "The living room… was just immaculate. It had this huge mirror over the fireplace and it was all wood. Like a log cabin kind of feel to it. Just gorgeous."

A few unique features of the building created memories for the Smith family. The many nooks and crannies were an ideal environment for games of hide-and-seek. "It was like a labyrinth," says Smith. He fondly recalls the hand-operated freight elevator at the back, and one of the oldest operational elevators in Memphis, still equipped with gate and all. "My kids loved to ride that kind of stuff." The Smith children weren't the

The Cronin, Baker & Tindall showroom featured the latest trends in lighting and plumbing fixtures. **Memphis Greets You.**

Cronin, Baker & Tindall

first youngsters to enjoy this sort of play, either. A Gruenberg grandchild once told Smith how they used to ride the freight elevator to the top floor, then let the rope go and shoot all the way down to the basement. "It would just take off. It never would crash because it had counterweights, so you could only go a certain speed," Smith cautions. Smith frequently discovered remnants of the building's former inhabitants. Once, as he tore down the wallpaper in his son's room, he came across a growth chart the Gruenbergs started back in the 1940s. It recorded their kids' growth up to the 1960s. One closet featured Hopalong Cassidy wallpaper.

Less visible signs of previous occupants were the unexplained bumps in the night. "I'm not saying it's haunted. But I'm not saying it's not haunted either," Smith says of the building. Since the apartment was above the business, he often attempted to find the source of any unusual sounds. "You'd hear weird noises. And it was one of those things where I would get up and search the building, thinking somebody's in the building." Smith insists he is a skeptic and likely to find an explanation for such happenings. However, there were a few "hair raising, goose bump moments" he simply could not explain, like the noise of a door slamming, yet when he investigated, all the doors in the building were open. "Of course there's been rumors of different people passing away in the building," Smith adds. Some of them lived in the building, while others worked there when they passed.

When asked about the current state of the property, Smith explains, "It's a hundred year old building. It needs some TLC." High utility bills and the typical limitations of a downtown location, such as lack of customer parking, prompted Sign Smiths to move from Madison Avenue. Being downtown sometimes had its thrills, though. "There was a club next door and a lot of times we'd have people twirling fire and hula-hooping out in the street out front," Smith describes, laughing. The building sat in a prime location for viewing fireworks at AutoZone Park. The family often watched the show from the parking lot or an open window.

Advance Rubber Stamps, now Sign Smiths, has changed in more ways than just location. The stamp industry itself developed into a very different business that contrasts sharply with the days of the Gruenbergs or the Davises. These days the company includes just the two brothers. "When Charlie [Hodges] took over for the Davises, he had ten employees; but he started introducing equipment that, as this piece would come in and somebody would leave, we wouldn't necessarily have to replace them right away or at all," says Smith.

When Advance Rubber Stamps began, each stamp and sign was hand-carved. Today's technological advancements mean the Smith brothers can operate a smaller, more efficient shop. "I can put $500 worth of stuff in the laser for thirty minutes and walk away and... go to the CNC router and set up a thousand dollar job that's going to run for thirty minutes... By the time I'm done with that the laser's done," he describes. "I'm not sitting here carving signs by hand anymore." Smith can now make ten flash stamps in the same amount of time it took to make a single old-fashioned polymer stamp.

Smith clearly has a love for the old ways

of doing things, even with all the new available technology. He discusses one piece of equipment the brothers had to leave behind when they moved from Madison Avenue. "The one that broke my heart, it was a [Gorton] pantograph machine. I heard that came off of a naval ship." The interesting detail about the machine was that its work in one spot actually happened on a larger scale on the other side. "It had a spindle with a router bit in it. I would have a letter that was made of metal and maybe a piece of plastic over here that I'm cutting. I'd trace the metal letter, and it would cut it out in plastic or a jig or something like that," he says

about the time-consuming process. The CNC router can now computerize this job with very little human involvement.

The hundred-year-old building that stands at 339 Madison Avenue stores more than the stamp industry's left-behind relics, now useless for modern business. The walls saw three families come and go, and listened in on decades of change in downtown Memphis. As it awaits new owners, the fireworks that follow summer baseball games will continue to light up the sky over its roof while concert music from W.C. Handy Park drifts by on the wind.

"IT WAS SUCH A MAGICAL TIME,

WHEN I WAS GROWING UP, TO GO DOWNTOWN

AS A YOUNG GIRL."   — VICKI JACKSON

Painting of 101, the address of a downtown condominium. New condos keep popping up in this area, now known for the arts and popular local restaurants. **Rebecca Phillips.**

LIVING BETWEEN THE LORRAINE AND THE ARTS IN DOWNTOWN MEMPHIS

The condo's yellow door with a simple "101" address is as unassuming as it gets, yet it represents the wave of prime urban dwellings that have popped up all over the area, and signals the rebirth of Downtown Memphis. The dwelling is situated across from the National Civil Rights Museum, formerly the Lorraine Motel. The smell of barbecue drifts on the smoke that rises from a nearby barbecue joint. The South Main Arts District, a phoenix of urban development, is within walking distance of the condo. From there, anyone can hop the trolley and ride to the downtown's other side for a dollar. This kind of urban lifestyle has only recently developed in Memphis after a long history of industry and emptiness.

The story of Memphis begins with the Chickasaw Indians, who lived on the Mississippi River bluffs centuries before any Europeans even laid eyes on the land. Hernando DeSoto was the first explorer to arrive in 1541. Others followed, including Sieur de LaSalle, who landed in 1682. Some trade developed along the river, and in 1796, Tennessee became a U.S. state. Official plans for the city of Memphis were drawn in 1819. The small city of fifty was comprised of just four blocks.

The city's growth came on the backs of German and Irish immigrants who constructed buildings and worked for the railroad. Because of its geographic location near the Mississippi River, Memphis was a hub for transportation and trade, making it a strategic area to control during the Civil War. Ten thousand citizens watched as Confederate and Union troops fought an intense naval battle over the city in 1862. The Union victory paved the way for an influx of former slaves, and increased the African-American population fourfold between 1860 and 1870. Although there were clashes between white and black populations, black politicians and public servants made strong gains in the Reconstruction era.

Memphis was almost lost to the yellow fever epidemic which plagued the city for more than ten years. Many fled. Eighty percent of those who stayed fell ill during the worst of the fever in 1878, and 25 percent of those people died. In the 1880s, the city established the first sewage system of its kind in the country; and the discovery of artesian wells provided fresh, clean water. Assisted by these developments, the fever finally ended and Memphis grew and prospered. Prosper it did, mostly through the benevolence of "King Cotton." Memphis was one of the busiest Southern cities by the mid-1900s.

Until 1850, what is now South Main was an entirely separate "suburb" called South Memphis, where wealthy families lived in mansions and single-family homes. As Memphis grew, Main Street became increasingly important for business and social life. "Going downtown" usually involved dressing up to spend the entire day shopping, eating lunch (perhaps dinner, too), or maybe catching a movie at one of the cinemas like The Majestic. Back then, Main Street was a busy twelve blocks between Court Square and Beale Street.

South Memphis changed entirely in the early 1900s with the addition of two major train stations, Central and Union Stations. The railroads made the area an attractive place for warehouses and distribution centers, like major movie studios MGM and Paramount. The railroad stations delivered up thousands of workers and passengers daily. With sidewalks full of customers, it is not hard to imagine how quickly the residential atmosphere gave way to commerce. Between 1910 and 1925, commercial buildings replaced mansions and homes, many of which still stand on South Main. Anyone who lived downtown at that time probably lived above his or her own store.

"It was such a magical time, when I was growing up, to go downtown as a young girl," Vicki Jackson recalls. When she turned twelve in the early sixties, her parents finally allowed her to catch the bus and go downtown with

friends. "My brother and I used to go all through the neighborhood just looking for soda bottles to pick up and cash in... and I would save up babysitting money. Back then if you had five, ten dollars you could go a long way and do a lot of fun things with that." Once they saved enough, they dressed in their coolest outfits and caught the bus. "The buildings were incredible. There was still traffic on the street and people walking up and down the sidewalks," she recalls, amazement for this special place still in her voice.

She describes a typical excursion, "The first place we would go would be the Blue Light Studio." For two dollars, the studio created a strip of glossy, softly lit, wallet-sized photographs that were cut apart and picked up at the end of the day. "While we were looking fresh we wanted to have those photos taken. And we weren't the only ones. That was a big,

MAIN ST. NORTH FROM McCALL ST.

View of North Main Steet from Mcall Steet, 1911. The Majestic, a well known theater for many years, is now a restaurant of the same name, decorated in an old cinema theme. **Memphis and Shelby County Room, Memphis Public Library and Information Center.**

big, big deal back then. Even entertainers would go there!" Jackson reminisces about how wonderful the photos looked – wonderful enough to keep going back, even in their twenties. "They could make the world's ugliest looking person look beautiful just by the way they took the photograph," she insists.

A familiar experience for a trip downtown was to dine at Britling's, the premier cafeteria in Memphis. "It was a big deal because you'd get your dessert first before you did anything else," Jackson laughs. Because the concept of a cafeteria was so new, and dining out was such a rarity back then, time spent at Britling's was like eating at a nice restaurant. "Then you had Kress, the dime store, and A. Schwab's, so those were two places we always hit," Jackson says, "Typically, we'd get a flavored soda because it was less expensive than a milkshake. We

were trying to make our money stretch as far as we could for the day!" They usually bought a little something from the store before they continued their big day out, often ending their time downtown with a movie at the Malco. Afterward, life went back to saving up in order to return.

Viewing a movie downtown was a pretty big deal in the forties and fifties. Except for special occasions, most people saw movies at neighborhood cinemas within walking distance of their homes. New movies screened downtown before they showed at these smaller neighborhood theaters. "If you wanted to see them first, you had to go downtown," says Stoy Bailey, who grew up behind his own neighborhood theater, the Lamar. He explains why there were so many movie theaters downtown, "The movie companies made the

Aerial view of downtown in February 1972, with the iconic "M" bridge over the Mississippi River under construction in the background. **Special Collections, University of Memphis Libraries.**

South Main Street downtown, looking north, 2014. **Jeremy Greene.**

movies... they built the theaters and that's how they distributed their films. So they all had theaters down there," he recalls, naming as many as six theaters open downtown at that time.

The department stores downtown were a major draw, even for working-class families like Jackson's. She remembers how exciting it was when her family went to Goldsmiths, though most of the time they only looked and did not buy anything. "Going to Goldsmiths was a really big deal... My mom would go there to buy a dress for a special occasion. They couldn't afford to buy all of our clothes there. But we loved to... walk around and look and see all the mannequins and their displays." Occasionally, a little extra money afforded a trip down to the bargain basement. "If we did buy something from Goldsmiths then we were glowing by the time we went to school on Monday morning,"

she says with a smile.

Downtown businesses largely depended on the railroads. A progressive decrease in train stops and the closure of Union Station in 1964, signaled disaster for downtown's economy. Dr. Martin Luther King, Jr.'s assassination in 1968, and the subsequent riots, practically emptied the area. Downtown became a ghost of its former self, filled with vacant buildings and deserted streets.

In 1976, President Gerald Ford inaugurated the Mid-America Mall, later renamed the Main Street Mall. The project failed in its attempt to save downtown, presumably because it shaped Main Street as a pedestrian-only area. The city resorted to an unusual strategy to bring in people and "mall" shoppers; they stopped tourists on the interstate and brought them to Main Street. Memphis remained virtually abandoned until a group of citizens banded together and developed a thriving downtown once again.

In the 1970s, master architect Jack Tucker began work on the first modernized residential building downtown. The Timpani Building on Union Avenue was named such because it was "banging the drum for Downtown." The group of visionaries who lived in the Timpani formed the core of what became the Downtown Neighborhood Association. They were soon joined by residents from other renovated historical buildings. The group served as downtown's active political arm, determined to maintain its unique atmosphere and to promote

the area's safety and security.

Robert McGowan and Annie Mahaffey awakened the South Main Arts District renaissance when they purchased a building as their home and art studio in 1982. Abandoned for decades, the area had low property costs and completely intact historical buildings, which created charming living and working space. With the opening of the National Civil Rights Museum in 1991 and the revival of Central Station in 1999, the nineties saw "anchors" come into the community. The trolley system was reinstated in 1993, complete with antique trolleys from Lisbon, Portugal and Melbourne, Australia. The Memphis College of Art

South Main and Calhoun Streets, 1940s. Arcade Restaurant is on the left. **Memphis and Shelby County Room, Memphis Public Library & Information Center.**

Graduate School came to South Main in 2010, assembled inside a converted warehouse. "This place has really enlivened in the last ten years," says local historian, Jimmy Ogle, reflecting on South Main's history.

The long-forgotten, beautiful, historic structures are more appreciated today. For many residents, building preservation is central to the revitalization of downtown. "There have been so many groups that have tried to preserve these buildings," Jackson says. "They used to have to fight harder a couple decades ago than they do now." She expresses her deep love for the architecture of the old buildings. "There's life in them to me... If the walls could speak, if the foundations could tell you about the feet that have walked on them... I think that's still why I love coming to Midtown and Downtown so much," she says, wrapped up in the memories and in awe of the history the buildings held onto for so many years.

Painting of the historic Arcade Restaurant sign. The sign stands proudly on the north side of the oldest restaurant in Memphis. **Rebecca Phillips.**

"I KEEP COMING BACK HERE BECAUSE OF THE CAMARADERIE AND THE FOOD. WHERE ELSE CAN YOU GO FOR $2.75?" — ERNIE BLUMFIELD

THE ARCADE, MEMPHIS' OLDEST RESTAURANT

The Paris Café began as just a tiny, wood framed diner with a potbelly stove and an icebox. In 1919, Greek immigrant Speros Zepatos turned that little building into the Arcade, now one of Downtown's most beloved restaurants. Zepatos named his restaurant after similar establishments he saw in New York and Atlanta, called "arcades." These places were akin to today's shopping mall – locations where people bought things or gathered for a meal. The day Zepatos threw open the doors for his first customers, he opened the door to his legacy, starting what would become Memphis' oldest restaurant.

In 1925, Zepatos tore down the original wooden structure and began to replace it with a seven-story hotel. "He always wanted to get into the hotel business," says Harry Zepatos, Jr. However, due to the looming threat of economic downturn he stopped construction on the hotel but preserved the restaurant. "They knew it [the Depression] was coming," Zepatos, Jr., says in admiration of his grandfather's business acumen. "In the middle of construction the economy was just taking a nosedive. So they didn't do it." Zepatos' new restaurant on the corner acted as an anchor for about a dozen rental properties on either side, and these tenants became a steady flow of diners. The storefront he created remains an iconic architectural element along South Main Street.

The restaurant thrived for decades, from the 1920s on up to the 1950s. Thousands of travelers, railway workers, and soldiers spilled out from the Central and Union train stations.

Hungry diners clogged the sidewalks at all hours and soon found their way into any of the eleven restaurants within view of the Arcade. One of these customers, Ernie Blumfield, chose the Arcade for his last meal in 1942, before he caught a train out of Memphis to fly a B-21 Bomber. "I keep coming back here because of the camaraderie and the food. Where else can you go for two dollars and 75 cents?" the 60-year-old asked a reporter in 1983.

The Arcade was open twenty-four hours a day, seven days a week, without fail. Not even a lock secured the door until the 1968 riots, after Martin Luther King, Jr.'s assassination. Zepatos, Jr., recalls that day, "My father and I were planting a tree at the house. They called and said, 'you gotta come down, they want us to close up.'" It took all night to close down the restaurant. "It'd never been closed. They'd never turned this stuff off... there was a lock [on the door] but nobody had the key. They had to get a locksmith to come down," Zepatos, Jr., recounts. Early the next morning his father received a call from the police who wanted him to come back and open up; they needed a place to eat while on twenty-four-hour duty. Zepatos gathered the employees and returned to the twenty-four-hour-a-day schedule. Although a city-wide curfew was in place, the Arcade stayed open to feed the police force that remained downtown all night.

The dream of hotel ownership was not laid to rest forever back in the 1920s. The Arcade Hotel, which Zepatos and son leased for over fifty years, once stood across from the Arcade Restaurant. Originally called the Winona, this little hotel first opened in 1914. Like the restaurant, it catered to railway workers and travelers. Rooms were cheap – just two dollars a night. All but seven of the thirty-one rooms shared a bathroom and only one had a private shower. During the latter half of the 1960s, nightly rates reached as high as thirty-five dollars a night. Most of its clientele were recent graduates looking for a job in Memphis. Zepatos, Jr., remembers he earned more money as a kid working at the hotel than across the street at the restaurant. He received tips at the hotel for running small errands. "You know a little kid carrying up their suitcase, they'll give you some money. Then they'll send you over here [the Arcade Restaurant] for a hamburger

and give you a little more money. At the end of the day I thought, 'This is great!'"

The Arcade Hotel eventually closed in 1983, but went on to have a new, albeit brief, life as a tourist attraction. Director Jim Jarmusch chose the Arcade Hotel as the setting for his cult classic, *Mystery Train*. In the film, three travelers, whose interconnected stories play out in Memphis, check into a decrepit old hotel. As Roger Ebert described in his review of the film, "this hotel is on life support." In fact, Memphis itself appears on life support in Jarmusch's movie. "The city seems forlorn and deserted: Vacant lots, boarded storefronts, hardly any traffic or pedestrians," Ebert wrote. Regardless, the film gave the hotel's interior a bit of a boost, as the

Arcade Restaurant entrance, 2014. It was once a 24-hour eatery, never locking its doors. **Jeremy Greene.**

lobby's original 1950s look was recreated for the movie scenes. The wrecking ball finally came for the old hotel in 1993. Restoration proved too expensive after vandalism and damage prompted the city to condemn the building.

The Arcade Restaurant's classic forties and fifties décor made it a perfect place to shoot scenes for *Mystery Train* and other films like *My Blueberry Nights*, *Walk the Line*, *Elizabethtown*, *21 Grams*, *The Client*, *The Firm*, and *Great Balls of Fire*. However, silver screen appearances did not automatically translate into a steady stream of diners. Some have called the Arcade a "barometer" for the rest of Downtown, and the eighties and nineties were tough on both. Some days the restaurant closed with a day's

take of just three hundred dollars. The popularity of Downtown waned when safety became a concern. Harry Zepatos was in his mid-sixties at the time and ready to retire. His son did well running a couple of Baskin Robbins ice cream stores, whereas the restaurant struggled. Consequently, he sold the Arcade to its longtime admirer Jacque Travis in 1995.

Travis knew her way around the restaurant business, having been general manager of the Butcher Shop downtown for over a decade. She added new cuisine to the Arcade's menu and live entertainment on Sunday afternoons. Her long-term plans included outdoor seating. She respected the history of the place, which Zepatos appreciated. The vintage décor stayed

Main Street in December 1943. A billboard for the Gayoso Hotel sits on the roof of the Arcade. **Memphis and Shelby County Room, Memphis Public Library and Information Center.**

(with a few fitting additions), along with the Arcade Hotel's lighting fixtures and the original 1945 milkshake mixers. Alas, her efforts were not enough to turn the business around. In 1996 a heartbroken Travis hung up a For Sale sign.

A pizza delivery truck appeared in front of the Arcade in 1997, and with it came the owner of one of the top pizza places in New Orleans, Colin Perel, and his father, Phil. Perel contemplated a second location for his highly rated New Orleans' Pie in the Sky when his father convinced him to toss pizzas at the Arcade instead. Initial plans involved a curtailed version of the Arcade's typical fare and a slow transition to pizzas and Italian sandwiches.

A family dispute after Phil Perel's death seemed to put Memphis' oldest restaurant in danger of closing its doors. In 2001, a two year court battle that threatened the restaurant's future finally ended. Although he emerged the victor, Colin Perel did not have the necessary funds to reopen and operate the Arcade. Perel put the restaurant up for sale. Zepatos, Jr., still owned the building and interviewed multiple potential owners. Most prospects had the talent to run a restaurant there but he wanted the place to maintain its character. All the while, his wife persistently asked, "Are you sure you don't want to do this?" The way she saw it, if any of these successful restaurateurs came in, he would likely never get a chance to return to the family business. In January 2002, Harry Zepatos, Jr., bought his family's restaurant back.

It almost seems like fate that Zepatos, Jr., would come back to the business where he grew up. He returned home after years pursuing other interests. At sixteen he asked his father

if he could, "go do something else." His dad laughingly asked him what he had in mind. "Man stuff," replied a young Zepatos, Jr., which led to a few years of work in the construction industry. When he attempted a return to the family restaurant, his father urged him to continue on his own path for a little while longer. Zepatos, Jr., received an engineering degree, followed by three years of high class travel with an architectural firm. "They insisted that we made a show," he says, recalling stopovers at the finest hotels and the huge tips his group left for their servers.

Zepatos, Jr., sits under the neon signs and 1950s décor, proud to have his grandfather's business back in the family. Currently, the street outside is experiencing a renaissance of sorts, and he plans to go along for the ride. "We need a bar... and those high chairs and tables so you can see the trolley," he says. Some days it can feel like "a zoo" at the Arcade. He envisions busy days in the future where customers sip mimosas and kids drink hot chocolate while waiting for a table. His two sons will likely join the business one day, too. They worked at the Arcade in the past and are eager to return, but for now Zepatos, Jr., encourages them to have their own adventures – like father like sons.

Today the Arcade is full of everyone from tourists to regulars. For decades the restaurant served meals to celebrities like Elvis and near-legendary regulars, who sit in the same seat and eat the same food year after year. Chris Collins keeps that tradition alive. He eats two eggs, bacon, and a side of fruit a few times a week. Like most regulars, he prefers to sit in the same place: the second or third seat at the counter,

An Arcade regular keeps his favorite mug at the restaurant. **Courtesy of Chris Collins.**

near the kitchen. Collins keeps a coffee cup with his name on it at the restaurant to ensure he drinks from the perfect mug. "The Arcade used to have smaller coffee cups but some time ago they changed over to larger ones. I wasn't a fan. It just so happened that my church downtown uses the same ones as the old cups. I lifted one to keep at the restaurant and put my name on it for safekeeping," Collins explains. Like most regulars, he has fears that if not for the Arcade, he "might not ever have received nourishment." He is another addition to the dozens of regulars before him, with dozens still to come, who all arrive at the Arcade for a little nourishment, both for the body and for the soul.

"IT WAS A MEETING PLACE. IDEAS WERE BORN,

PEOPLE CAME AND WENT, PEOPLE TALKED ABOUT

THEIR FAMILIES, SHARED HOLIDAYS TOGETHER

GETTING THEIR HAIR DONE FOR THANKSGIVING."

— SHARON ANDREINI

Painting of the Beauty Shop sign reflection against the inside wall. The restaurant's sign and personality reflect that of a 1950s beauty shop. **Rebecca Phillips.**

MIDTOWN'S TIMELESS BEAUTY: THE BEAUTY SHOP

"Anything you wanted to do you could do in Cooper-Young. They had a grocery store, gas stations, furniture stores, an old-fashioned drug store... You could walk wherever you wanted to go," Sharon Andreini fondly remembers. One of the most happening places in the neighborhood was Atkins Beauty and Barbershop. "It was *the* place to get your hair done," she says of her father's shop. Bemis Atkins' unique two-in-one shop was a perfect fit for Cooper-Young's atmosphere when he opened it back in the mid-1940s. The shop has captured the neighborhood's essence ever since.

Both men and women got their hair done at Atkins. It was simple: Men went to the left, and women went to the right. A wall divided the space between them to avoid seeing unseemly things like a woman sitting in her curlers or a man lathering up for an old-fashioned shave. Atkins had a shoeshine station as well, just to make sure everyone looked sharp from head to toe. The place was always upbeat and noisy with more than just the constant click of scissors. "It was a meeting place. Ideas were born, people came and went, people talked about their families, shared holidays together getting their hair done for Thanksgiving," Andreini recalls.

A number of celebrities frequented Atkins throughout the years. Isaac Hayes brought his girlfriend there, and singer Al Green's mother got her wigs at Atkins. Priscilla Presley chose the first booth when she dropped by for her signature bouffant. Andreini remembers her visits, "She would always come in the back door because it was less of an ordeal for her." Robin Tucker, who would later lease the building, had an aunt who did hair at Atkins. Sometimes Elvis would call and request that she come to Graceland to do Priscilla's hair on a Saturday night. Her aunt would blow off his request because she always had plans to go dancing or do something else on a weekend night. Whether famous or a nearby resident, one was sure to leave with the latest gossip and a great hairdo. "Every time you went in there it was full of people. Under the hairdryer, with their heads in the sink, getting their nails done. There was always a hubbub," recalls Andreini, often found spinning on the barber chairs as a girl, and refusing to stop when the adults warned her she would get sick.

The barber and beauty shop wasn't the first new thing Atkins brought to the area in the 1940s. He also introduced southerners to the batter-fried hotdog, the Pronto Pup, when he brought his first concession stand to the Mid-South Fair in 1946. "This is a trademarked franchise item, Pronto Pup, and it was born right there on that corner... My dad was the first to bring it to this part of the United States. Before that it was up in Oregon," Andreini explains. He refurbished and painted his stands in the corner building near his barbershop. The company grew to seventeen stands by 1987; but a stroke took him away from running either business.

Andreini was more interested in the food business than in doing hair, so longtime Atkins beautician, Ruth Cook, took over the beauty and barbershop. Then, in the mid-nineties, Robin Tucker, a hair stylist known for creating vintage

Intersection of Cooper Street and Young Avenue in the 1940s. Atkins Beauty and Barber Shop on left.
Memphis and Shelby County Room, Memphis Public Library & Information Center.

looks, unknowingly returned to her roots. Tucker describes her method as, "taking elements of the past and adding pieces to it." This statement may describe her style philosophy, but it also says everything about how she treated Atkins Beauty and Barbershop. As soon as Tucker leased the building to set up her own studio, she called her mom to share the happy news, and learned she was in Atkins before and had forgotten all about it. Tucker's mother worked as the receptionist there while pregnant with her. As a small child, Tucker sat at her aunt's feet while she styled Priscilla Presley's hair. "For me it was, I'd just have to say supernatural... It's amazing to think you started in a place, you don't remember it, come back, and you just randomly decide to do hair... It seemed like it was already predestined," Tucker says about the whole experience.

Tucker appreciated everything about her new space. The authentic retro décor echoed the fifties vintage style she was known for giving clients. She freshened up the walls with green paint and added some Elvis photos to the walls, along with some of her own work. One day she removed the front window so eight people could bring in the 1958 Mercedes Benz that served as the reception desk.

She also admired the former Atkins employees who still worked in the space. She may have changed the business' name to Hollywood Designs, but barber Riley Shumaker stayed on at the front, and Ruth Cook kept her "blue hairs" in the back. Tucker worked in the center of the shop. "I think my greatest experience there was walking in to two people who were intimidated, thought I was going to fire them, ask them to leave, and then we actually became really good friends," says Tucker.

Even though they all found a mutual respect for each other, there certainly was a culture clash between the fifties era stylists and Tucker, who traveled extensively and had been a stylist for movie stars and famous musicians. Most of Shumaker and Cook's clients never left Memphis, did not go to movie theaters, and did not drink. Tucker always admired Cook's ability to do so many shampoo and sets, the main service Cook's clients requested. "She did ten blue hairs an hour and rocked them out!" Tucker also recalls a time when Shumaker was hospitalized. She took care of his clients at seven dollars a cut and gave him all the money when he was released from the hospital. She loved the loyalty of Cook's and Shumaker's clients, noting that they never missed their regular appointments.

The fourteen to sixteen hour days finally caught up with Tucker. After four years,

The vintage car that served as Robin Tucker's reception desk at Hollywood Designs. **Robin Tucker.**

she closed Hollywood Designs and left the charming little beauty shop in the hands of restaurateur Karen Carrier. Like Tucker, Carrier felt a kind of supernatural pull to the old Atkins shop. She ran her downtown restaurant, Automatic Slims, for seventeen years before she wanted to branch out in 2000 and add a new place that had a neighborhood-like feeling. "I came into Cooper-Young... it was pouring down rain and the door to this space was

cracked open and there was a For Rent sign in the window," Carrier remembers, "There was a woman in here saying she was going to open a furniture store. So I just took the number down and called the landlord and she told me what the rent was and I asked her if I could come over and give her some money down. I just basically rented it that day."

Carrier found the original beauty shop décor incredibly charming. "When I saw it and walked in here and felt the good feeling I felt, I was like, oh I gotta have this,'" she says with a smile. She kept as many of the original fixtures as possible and made minimal adjustments. The only substantial changes made were moving the hair washing sinks to the bar, reupholstering the seats, and replacing the ceiling. Even the hairdryers and other features like the glass dividing walls remain. Diners can even settle into the same booth Priscilla Presley did back in the day. Carrier remembers the day Presley came in for lunch and requested to sit in the first booth again. "It brought back a lot of memories for her, you could tell," she says.

Even though she kept much of it the same, it still took Carrier a year to refit the beauty shop into a restaurant. While they worked on the front of the building, Ruth Cook continued to take care of her clients, and only left when

construction started on the kitchen in the back. The Beauty Shop finally opened its doors in 2002, with a name that serves as a nod to the place's rich history and past. "The first year I was open there were so many people who came in here and said, 'oh I used to get my hair done here, or my grandmother used to get her hair done here, or my aunt used to…' so apparently this place was *rockin'* in its time,'" Carrier observes. Like those who came before her, Carrier's love for the little shop's history shines through every choice she made with her restaurant. Year after year this little corner of Cooper-Young lives on as *the* place to be.

The intersection of Cooper Street and Young Avenue, 2014. **Eric Swartz.**

Painting of Joe's Wines and Liquors' iconic Roto-Sphere sign in the daytime. The sign spans 20 feet from one of the neon arms to the other. **Rebecca Phillips.**

THE SPINNING LIGHTS OF JOE'S WINES AND LIQUORS

The Sputnik, as it's known around town, is always ready for a close-up. As one of Memphis' most iconic signs, its rotating neon arms have been photographed, painted, and artistically captured for decades. The Sputnik is synonymous with Joe's Wines and Liquors, and figures prominently in the store's history and growth.

Before the days of the Joe's, one of the first Piggly Wiggly grocery stores occupied the building. The back side was Peter Pan's Pantry convenience store, which eventually closed. The liquor business took over the front of the building in the early sixties. Joe's original owner, Joe Solomito, installed the neon rotating sign just in time for the Grand Opening in 1962. In fact, a picture of the striking signage was prominently featured in the Grand Opening ad. Until the early seventies Joe's was farther east than any other liquor store, and one can only imagine the need to create a "destination" using unique signage.

The spinning Roto-Sphere threw sweeps of color over Poplar Avenue and demanded attention. This massive sphere with aluminum "arms" rotates in three directions simultaneously: It rotates around itself while its two hemispheres counter-rotate around a 90 degree axis. An early sales brochure states, "the three-dimensional motions give a depth and character which is unequaled by any other form of animation."

This highly unique design was the brainchild of the late Warren Milks, a down-to-earth inventor and sign shop owner in Bossier City, Louisiana. His home was fitted with tiny, neon "potted" plants and neon religious sayings, a simple dwelling for the man who graced America's roadways with the most dynamic and eye-catching signs ever created.

Contrary to popular belief, Milks did not think about the Sputnik satellite when he created this signature design. Some have speculated his inspiration was *Playhouse 90*, or perhaps a commercial for children's toys, or Christmas ornaments. Milks could not recall. All he knew was that he was watching television one day and something sparked a light bulb moment. What followed was the creation and production of approximately 234 Roto-Spheres between 1960 and 1971.

Local sign shops around the country ordered Roto-Spheres directly from Milks' sign shop in Bossier City, where he personally produced each one. Their colorful life began with a simple coat of white primer and a card from Milks suggesting what colors to paint them. The finished product would arrive in two packages, one for the steel ball and one for the arms. The customer then made their own final color selections for the paint and the neon.

While we typically call a Roto-Sphere (and its sister concepts the Turn-Star and Roto-Ring) a sign, Milks wanted it be an attention-getter. "Advertisers are constantly seeking new means and methods of attracting attention in this high speed civilization. The buying public has had their 'sign appetite' jaded by numerous electrically lighted signs and displays on the world's busy highways – and the competition

New!

Turn-Star

Roto-Sphere

most modern concepts of

SPECTACULAR *lighting application*

The cover image of a Turn-Star and Roto-Sphere brochure. **Courtesy of Debra Jane Seltzer.**

for the travelling [sic] public's eye has become terrific." Even in today's world his sales copy rings true.

Much of the information about the Sputnik's inventor would be lost without Debra Jane Seltzer. Seltzer became a leading historian of road signs like the Sputnik after she completed extensive research on historic signs and documented them during cross-country road trips. She shares information like maps and photos with a larger community of sign enthusiasts. Seltzer visited with Milks a few times in Bossier City before he passed away in 2012. On her last trip, she drove this relatively unknown inventor to a coffee shop with Wi-Fi. Seltzer popped open her laptop and showed

Milks how much people loved his signs. He slowly read his fans' excited comments on the pictures of the signs he once sent all over the U.S. His amazement and disbelief were palpable; before that moment, he had no idea how much joy his signs brought to others.

The Joe's Sputnik is one of only an estimated seven remaining Roto-Spheres in operation. This giant sign spans 20 feet from one end of the neon arms to the other. Making it rotate again was no small feat. Not only did the mechanics have to be adjusted to keep it turning smoothly, the paint and neon also needed an overhaul.

Enter Brad Larson, the current owner of Joe's, who purchased the business in 1998 from Walter Wilkenson. Larson's earliest intention for Joe's was to restore the Sputnik. He wanted the sign to work and "work right." Larson was immediately surprised by customers who constantly asked when he would restore the sign. His response was, "Maybe if you put something, a dollar, in this pot here, we'll get it done." Accordingly, customers began leaving change in a collection jar on the counter.

A local Memphis band, Crash Into June, approached Larson about doing a fundraiser for the restoration. Neil's Music Room (formerly at Madison and McLean) was the ideal partner to host the event. Before it burned down in 2011, the bar was a mainstay for local musicians who needed a place to play in town. Local musician and tourism personality, Memphis Jones, recalls the fundraiser with a joyous laugh, "Joe's sign had been in disrepair for a long time. A great friend of mine named Clay Combs was leading a power pop group called Kitchens and

Joe's Roto-Sphere sign in motion at night. This sign is one of an estimated seven Roto-Spheres in operation. **Jeremy Greene.**

Bathrooms. This was part of that... power pop scene in Memphis. So Kitchens and Bathrooms and my band, we were called the Moves, and another band called Crash Into June, we put on an event there... It was huge. It was great!" Between the music, the amount of t-shirts sold, and auction funds, the event raised twelve thousand dollars.

The restoration involved quite a bit of trial and error. The internal mechanics had to be completely reworked, so it took a few years to figure out exactly how to reconfigure the system. The Roto-Spheres' original workings has been debated as much as the design's inspiration. Some suggested Milks used car parts to create the iconic rotating motion, yet Milks always contended he used a gear system.

Jeff Balton of Precision Sign Company worked with his father on Joe's Sputnik for several years, and kept it turning throughout the seventies until it went dormant from about 1978 to 1994. He states the sphere rotated with a 1930s rear end differential bolted onto two car axles. The clutch-type rotation system would often slip out of gear in high winds. The system was difficult to maintain even after reworking it during the restoration process. Larson recalls an early test of the new system, "Once it got going we were slinging neon into the middle of Poplar Avenue. Nobody got hurt, thank God." Each tube of neon is now firmly secured with eight wires while an electric motor keeps it spinning.

In 1999, Larson invited the Memphis community to celebrate the Sputnik's restoration. The "Re-launch the Sputnik Party"

drew over 500 people. Fireworks shot from the roof and a dry ice machine enhanced the celebratory atmosphere. "The guy who did the pyrotechnics for KISS back then lived in Memphis and he came out and put on a small pyrotechnic show," Larson fondly recalls.

Larson has no plans of letting the Sputnik go dark under his watch. "It's my spinning Corvette," he explains, "That's about as much money that's gone into it. I'll never own one, but I get to look at it." To recreate a Roto-Sphere like Joe's Sputnik today would cost something in the range of fifty thousand dollars. Some state laws now prohibit the use of rotating neon signs, so stores like Joe's must seek special permission to fully utilize these historic signs.

Taking on a massive restoration of the Sputnik, or Roto-Sphere as it is technically called, was not enough for Joe's current owner, Brad Larson. He expanded the store in 2009, and took over the boarded up rear portion of the building. The Sputnik's influence is apparent in the design choices John Harrison Jones Architects made for the new interior. Elements throughout the store, like funky metal panels, reflect the "mid-century character" of the neon sign outside.

Every year more and more of these historic creations disappear from our roadways. For now at least, weary travelers can find their way to Memphis by way of the neon light from this "spectacular lighting application" in the otherwise unassuming parking lot of Joe's Wines and Liquors.

Painting of Casey's Motel sign. The sign remains standing in front of vacant hotel rooms with locked doors and boarded windows. **Rebecca Phillips.**

SCANDAL AND MAYHEM AT CASEY'S MOTEL

Newspapers did not feature articles raving about fancy food, amazing turndown service, or a knowledgable concierge at Casey's Motel. Rather, they contained pieces about very real problems with heists, mayhem, murder, and prostitution. The story of this doomed lodging place began on 1365 Dunn Road at the Rose Court Motel. A thirties era postcard depicts the motel as a line of squat, brick buildings. Inside, the business housed double beds with peaceful blue spreads and a small seating area. The location was just five miles from Downtown Memphis, perfect for the Rose Court Motel's business philosophy of "Tourists–Travelers–Strictly."

The Rose Court Motel became Casey's Motel after the business moved to 1585 Bellevue, also known as Hwy 51, where its sign now sits in front of an empty building. This stretch of road was also officially named Elvis Presley Boulevard in 1971 because it runs right up to Graceland. Although a hub for tourist activity, the strange history of Casey's Motel is representative of the challenges to overcome in this historic area of Memphis.

A late 1930s postcard featuring Rose Court, which later became Casey's Motel. **Courtesy of Birch Harms.**

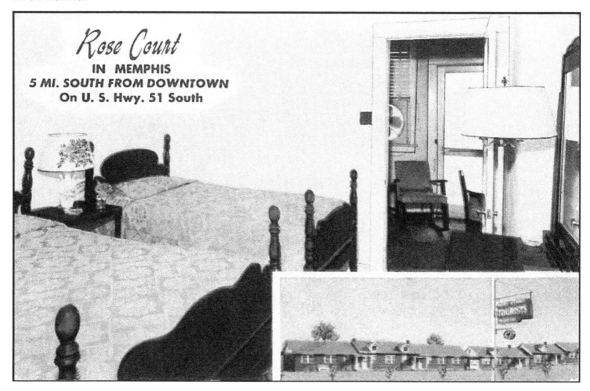

*Casey's Motel sign in 2013, representing a place once describing itself as "one of the finest." **Jeremy Greene.***

A 1950s era postcard for Casey's describes it as "one of the finest." The sign appears to be a brightly lit neon welcoming visitors into a courtyard surrounded by single-story yellow buildings. The back of the postcard describes the motel as, "less than fifteen minutes from the loop district," "Air-Conditioned," and "Convenient to Good Food." These amenities included television, all for seven to ten dollars a night.

By the seventies, Casey's was no stranger to holdups and masked bandits. One heroic woman made news with the headline, "Hotel Clerk No Fall Guy." Around 12:30 a.m. in August, 1971, a man asked front desk clerk Etta Johnson about a room. Instead of pulling out a wallet to pay for the room, the man drew a gun. Rather than give him the cash, she quickly "dropped to the floor and pushed the alarm."

The armed robber immediately fled.

In April 1976, a very strange robbery case appeared under the headline, "Tables Turned." Two screaming women ran into Casey's Motel lobby at 5:00 a.m., and claimed they had been robbed. When police arrived, a male guest stated the women were the actual thieves. The guest explained he had, "taken the two women to his room as 'guests,' and while he was in the bathroom the pair took $450 from his trousers and fled." Once police searched the women, they found the missing money. All three were arrested and subsequently investigated by the "larceny squad."

The biggest crime case connected to Casey's Motel was tied to Nashville. In November 1973, Nashville was rocked by the murder of two country music stars. Early in the month, Grand Ole Opry performer, David "Stringbean" Akeman, and his wife were found dead at their home in a rural area north of Nashville. The banjo player was famous for appearances on *Hee Haw*, a television program that showcased country music. This shocking homicide was soon followed by the murder of Jimmy Widener, another Opry regular.

Widener, a rhythm guitarist with Hank Snow's Rainbow Ranch Boys Band, and Mildred Hazelwood of California, were found in an alleyway of North Nashville, shot in an apparent robbery. A few nights later, a call from Memphis provided a break in the case. A "very neatly dressed" man attempted to buy a plane ticket to San Francisco at the American Airlines office inside the Peabody-Sheraton Hotel. Management was alerted to the transaction when he tried to pay for the ticket with Widener's credit card.

The tip led law enforcement to three suspects holed up at Casey's Motel. Two of the men were tricked into appearing at the front office. The third man engaged in a shootout with police from the motel room, but after "about 20 shots" were exchanged and tear gas was emitted into the room, the man "crawled out." Memphis police recovered five weapons from the room and located Widener's 1966 Continental, abandoned downtown just before the men took a cab to Casey's Motel.

Even though the killers were caught and jailed, these homicides completely changed Nashville's country music scene. Before the murders, stars worried little about crime affecting them. After the slayings, "Country stars now needed walls, security and protection beyond a pistol shoved into a battered old bag. Suddenly, things that had been normal for country musicians — like living in unsecured neighborhoods or drinking with fans and admirers at Tootsie's — seemed dangerous."

Robbery, kidnapping, or murder did not prove to be Casey's undoing, although crime certainly surrounded it. Instead, it was prostitution. Shawn Nichols encountered one such working girl at Casey's. Nichols wired several hourly rate motels in the nineties and picked up a side job at Casey's. He got an unexpected call on the job as he installed vents, vanity lights, and smoke detectors in every motel bathroom. "One day while working in one of the rooms, the phone rang. I answered, thinking it was probably the front office wanting something – it would not have been the first time they called me. A female was on the other end. 'When are you going to come see me?' she asked straightaway." Nichols recalls fumbling for an answer. "'Huh?' was all I managed." The woman on the other end of the line told him to look out the door. "I did and of course it was a prostitute, living in a room on the other side of the courtyard. Young and very pretty. Me, I blushed and ran back to work. She probably laughed and did the same. She never called again and I finished up soon after that."

Prostitution plagued the community around the hotels on this historic road, "They [prostitutes] are usually strolling and flagging down vehicles near that other bane of area residents: that cluster of semi-fenced-in, hourly rate motels." Casey's Motel temporarily shut down in November 2002, due to residents' complaints and thirty-three prostitution arrests since January of that year. The motel was allowed to reopen under certain conditions. They could not rent a room to known prostitutes, be associated with illegal activities, or lease a room more than one time in 24 hours. The owners risked jail time and fines if they did not comply with these orders.

The owners and community remained divided after the closure. The motel owners' attorney insisted "his clients were 'embarrassed' by the shutdown." The attorney revealed the owners would renovate the facilities to attract a "higher caliber of customer." Area residents, however, were dubious that a better looking motel would change anything and felt the illegal activities would simply continue.

Today, Casey's Motel sits abandoned on Elvis Presley Boulevard, a street with its own history and past. Before it was Elvis Presley Boulevard,

Casey's Motel shoot out, November 1973. **Special Collections, University of Memphis Libraries.**

the street was known as: "The Plank Road, The Hernando Road, Mississippi Boulevard, Jefferson Davis Highway, U.S. 51 South, and Bellevue." It began as an Indian trail running from Memphis to Hernando, Mississippi. A more official road with wooden planks and timbers was created in 1841. The planks were replaced with gravel in 1880, and "many people complained the gravel was hard on their horses' shoes."

The decision to name the road in honor of Memphis' most famous entertainer met with mixed response. The family expressed a sense of honor regarding the proposal. Martin Lacker, chairman of the board for Memphis Music, Inc., stated he felt, "the world has honored him [Elvis]. The rest of the country has honored him. I just feel its time Memphis honored him." The Memphis Area Chamber of Commerce supported the proposal due to a study they performed which indicated Graceland would be Memphis' "second largest tourist attraction after the Mississippi River."

Opposition came from business owners on the street. One physician presented a petition

Crime scene officer checking luggage while another inspects a pistol found in the suspects' room at Casey's Motel. **Special Collections, University of Memphis Libraries.**

with 193 signatures from 73 businesses on the street who were opposed to the name change. He was quick to point out the "group had no objection to Mr. Presley," rather, they appreciated the history and resonance that "South Bellevue" had in Memphis. Their objection to the new name centered on Presley's image of "gaiety, music, entertainment, and the lighter side of life," which was in sharp contrast to the "image of the quiet, old name of South Bellevue." Nevertheless, the ordinance passed and the street's name was indeed changed.

The name change precipitated an unexpected new criminal element to the area. City officials replaced street signs that featured Elvis' name as often as three times a month because of souvenir seekers. In the days following Presley's death, every road sign (114 in total) was stolen. Forty more signs were taken a little under a year after his death. In 1978, one souvenir seeker hacksawed the sign pole and shoved the whole thing into her car. Police spotted the ten-foot haul and put it back where it belonged. Placing street signs fourteen feet high on utility poles did little to discourage all thieves. "The extra four-foot climb hasn't deterred real Elvis lovers," a 1978 news report stated.

Major changes continue to happen in the community near Graceland. In 2008, state and local officials met in Memphis to discuss much needed improvements to Elvis Presley Boulevard, the "spine of the Whitehaven community." The project began in 2009 and covers three miles of this iconic street. The undertaking will enhance lighting and signage, and address infrastructure issues by widening intersections, repaving the road, and improving drainage. In his 2013 article, "Road to Graceland," Associated Press reporter, Adrian Sainz described Elvis Presley Boulevard as, "a mile's worth of empty businesses, vacant lots, crooked utility poles, crumbling sidewalks, poor lighting and drab landscaping." Lodging and dining options are nothing more than budget motels and fast food. Improvements will not just benefit tourists; the project is also designed to improve the quality of life and increase business opportunities in the Whitehaven area. The 43 million dollar project will be completed in 2017, and will usher in another stage of Elvis Presley Boulevard's history.

Painting of the Drink-N-Drag dancing girl sign. This sign is part of a collection of similar dancing lady signs. **Rebecca Phillips.**

DRINK-N-DRAG: THE LADY IN RED

The blonde lady scantily clad in a red neon dress is shrouded in as much rumor and mystery as the industry she represents. Her enigmatic smile remains through any kind of weather. High-heeled, red go-go boots complete her pinup girl look. Although she stands just blocks from where Elvis recorded at historic Sun Studio, she figures more prominently in the seedier side of Memphis history. She is frozen in time, mid-shake on the exterior wall of Drink-N-Drag at 616 Marshall Avenue. Before her stint at this particular nightclub, she was spotted in quite a few other places around town.

Originally created around 1985 by a sign maker who specialized in neon, this lady in red had five other likenesses. He built the first two dancing ladies for Danny Owens' original strip club on Airways. "They were basically made inverted. One would be looking one way and one would be looking the other way," explains their creator. The other four girls appeared on two large billboards at Airways and I-240.

The dancing ladies' construction was not the end of the story. These six ladies returned to the shop for repairs quite often. "He [Owens] had a lot of enemies in town. Somebody started shooting the ladies on those two billboards to try to break the neon and make it go out." Owens would commission the shop make more neon right away in hopes of eventually catching the perpetrators. "I probably made twenty sets of neon that went on them," the sign maker says.

The dancing ladies were so popular another strip club on Summer Avenue imitated them. "They put neon on them and tried to make them dance, but they didn't stay up very long," the original signs' creator explains. Alex McPeak remembers these copycats very clearly. "One of the most memorable signs from my childhood was the huge, neon dancing girls sign at what is now the Gold Club at Summer and White Station by the I-40/240 split... I always gaped at the huge neon dancers shaking it for the passing cars, while my mother admonished me for the questions I asked about them."

The original signs would have cost about three thousand dollars each. They were skillfully made from heavy, welded aluminum and glass with neon inside. Their inventor also designed their costumes, fashioning each girl's attention-grabbing dress and matching boots. "It's all called neon but there's two kinds of gas," the sign maker explains. Neon is an amber red color, while the other gas, argon, is blue. The color of each dancing lady depended on the combination of the tube's color and the gas inside. He explains, "You take a tube that looks white when it's turned off. But the inside would be green phosphor. If you pumped that green tube with neon, it would burn orange. If you pumped that green tube with argon, it would make green."

Suffice it to say, the blonde lady got around in her day. She made a few cameo appearances in *The Rainmaker*, the 1997 John Grisham adaptation shot on location in Memphis. One online reviewer said, "Memphians will easily recognize many of the sites, from Court Square and the Pinch district to The Med and the Shelby County Courthouse. (And the Las Savell jewelry store gets priceless free advertising.)"

Next to the fictitious law office is a place Memphians would know in a heartbeat: the infamous Danny's. Our lady in red and a friend flank the red letters which spell "Danny's" on the roof.

The film's art department created this "Danny's" as a nod to one of Memphis' most well-known strip clubs. A 1982 *Memphis Press-Scimitar* article shows the real Danny's, once located on Airways Boulevard, with the same signage depicted in the movie. The club's namesake, Danny Owens, was a shadowy figure in the Memphis strip club industry. Allegations of criminal activity and seedy business dealings abounded until he finally landed in federal prison in 1992.

The only one of her group who remains in the public eye, the lady in red presided over 616 Marshall for an undisclosed number of years. Before its current incarnation as an LGBT-friendly club, the space was a rock concert hall and dance club, a topless bar, and perhaps even more, depending on who does the telling. In the 1990s, Nathan Rosengarten operated Club Six-1-Six (sometimes referred to as Club 616) in this space, and featured mostly live rock

Danny's strip club as it appeared in the 1997 film The Rainmaker. **Special Collections, University of Memphis Libraries, photo by Sandy Felsenthal.**

performances, although The Chippendales performed there. Occasionally a "suspension team" performed, exposing their numerous piercings, often in places typically clothed in everyday life.

In 2005, Jerry Westlund purchased the property for $640,000 from Ralph Lunati, a big shot in the strip club industry. Westlund opened Downtown Dolls that same year and immediately ran into controversy. Disputes

Drink-N-Drag sign at the entrance to a club at 616 Marshall Avenue. **Jeremy Greene.**

over county and city ordinances, alcohol laws, and what actually went on in the club made headlines month after month. A 2007 news article described the place as "Memphis' only exotic dance club that, technically, doesn't operate as a strip club under city law."

The "grand plans" Westlund claimed to have for the club never materialized. Instead, signs for phantom venues like Off Beale Live and The Tenderloin steakhouse lined the building's walls. Anyone trying to open the door to the "restaurant" would find it had no handle. One visitor recalls his visit to Downtown Dolls saying "the club was so dead, the girl at the front waived the cover fee. A lone woman danced on stage to a room full of empty tables while the bartender restocked the bar coolers with bottles of Budweiser... as I exited Downtown Dolls to an empty Marshall Avenue, I knew the infamous scene in Memphis had been changed, and possibly ended, forever."

Downtown Dolls started catering to a

One of two additional dancing girl signs in the basement of Drink-N-Drag. **Courtesy of Jeffrey Smith.**

different crowd on New Year's Eve in 2010 when it became Club Spectrum, also known as the "Rainbow Church." In 2013 the venue changed its name to Drink-N-Drag. Clubbers enter through doors situated beneath a pair of neon legs. As the name promises, inside are sweet cocktails and late night drag shows. The bar is decorated with several large, white lips and a waterfall spills down from one wall. A round platform with a pole that rises to the ceiling serves as the room's centerpiece. "Drink-N-Drag is exactly what the name suggests, but what it doesn't tell you is how inviting and eager the employees are to introduce a new guest, like myself, to the art of pole dancing," says Erin Marie Adelman, a recent first time visitor. "I was apprehensive with the whole pole dancing thing, but once I got on that stage the instructor/dancer made me feel like 'I got this,' even though it couldn't be further from the truth!" Saturday nights bring large enough crowds to open up two adjoining rooms, one as a lounge area and the other for dancing.

Three other dancing ladies, similar in style but with different dress colors, rest in the basement of Drink N' Drag. Never aging or wrinkling, they quietly await another moment in the spotlight. Like all good gossip, details of Danny's original neon dancing girl's life is open to speculation. While no one will ever know all her secrets, everyone can imagine the riches she'd make from a tell-all memoir – if only she could write one.

"I SAW A LOT OF MOVIES THERE DURING

THOSE YEARS. EVERY ELVIS MOVIE RELEASED."

— CONNIE KNIGHT

Painting of Lamar Theater, which transitioned from screening family-friendly movies to playing adult films. **Rebecca Phillips.**

THE LAMAR THEATER: A NEIGHBORHOOD CINEMA

The doors to the Lamar Theater officially swung open on November 29, 1926. The movie screened for this grand event? *The Campus Flirt*, a silent black and white comedy that premiered two months earlier in New York City. A brand new Wurlitzer organ supplied music and sound effects for the film. The Twilight Serenaders also performed.

The presence of a Wurlitzer organ meant the Lamar was a top-notch cinema in the silent film era. Before the Rudolph Wurlitzer Company supplied organs to neighborhood theaters, most movies were accompanied by a single piano or, if moviegoers were lucky, a pit orchestra. Technological advances in the early 1900s transformed a traditional organ, like those used in churches, into a sound effects machine. The "Unit Orchestra" reproduced sounds like a train whistle, a ringing phone, and even "played" other instruments, like a trumpet or a drum. In the year the Lamar Theater opened, Wurlitzer shipped out an organ a day, but the 1927 film *The Jazz Singer*, the first to include sound, changed the game entirely. As more and more movies incorporated sound, organs lost popularity. Most theaters installed speaker systems rather than organs by the mid-1930s.

On Friday nights adults would go to the Lamar Picture Show, as it was called back then. On Saturdays it was the kids' territory. A typical Saturday included news, a cartoon, a serial, and two feature films. Serials were short, three to five minute episodic stories with dramatic plot lines featuring characters like Batman or the Lone Ranger. Kids were anxious to get back to the movies the next week to see what happened to their favorite heroes. Wilma Bickers recalls the serials with love, "I think I went as much for the serial as I did the movies. Frankly, I doubt any of us knew what the features would be, and we did not really care." Still, she had her favorites. For a serial it was *Fu Manchu*, with *Hopalong Cassidy* as her preferred western feature. Concessions figure strongly in Bickers' memories of the theater. "First thing when you entered the door after buying your ticket was to get an all-day Holloway caramel sucker (which nearly pulled the fillings out of your teeth) and really did last throughout the entire movie and beyond." Occasionally the draw of popcorn was too strong. "Sometimes I selected popcorn, which you could smell cooking even while standing in line to get your ticket," she recalls.

Like other kids in the neighborhood, Barry Pruette waited anxiously all week for Saturday to come. "On Saturdays I cut grass all morning on Felix to have money for the show, popcorn and candy," he recalls. For a dime he could get into the theater in time for the 2:00 p.m. start time. Pruette was thrifty with his Saturday spending. "My first little girlfriend was Shirley King and I always met her inside so I wouldn't have to pay," he says. His parents owned Breathrick Cleaners across the street from the theater. After a long day's work they joined him at the movies. "My parents closed the cleaners at 9:00 and then joined me for the last show. I could work my feet between the arm rest and sleep in my Mother's lap." For his twelfth birthday the young boy went to the theater

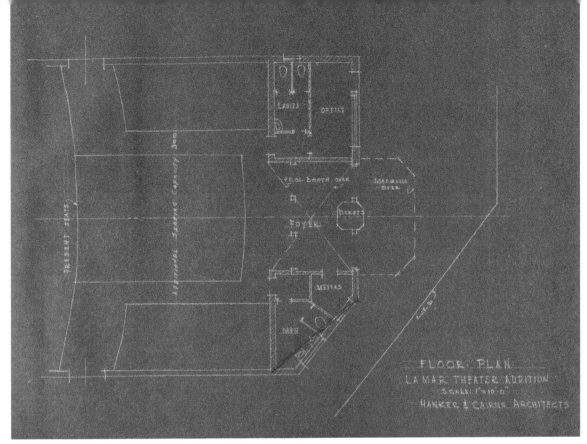

A 1935 floor plan for the interior of the Lamar Theater. **Memphis and Shelby County Room, Memphis Public Library and Information Center.**

alone, bravely planning to watch *The Mummy's Hand*. He missed quite a bit of the film. "I was so scared that I got under the seat on the back row!" Pruette remembers.

Stoy Bailey lives and works a stone's throw from the derelict theater. In fact, his home office occupies the room in which he was born. He fondly recalls the long Saturdays of movie watching at the Lamar. "For a quarter, back in the forties, you'd get your ticket into the theater, you'd get a box of popcorn, you'd get a candy bar, and go in and watch the movie," he reminiscences. In order to get into the movie, Bailey had to give his ticket to the collector at the door. One collector in particular, called Sheriff, made a lasting impression. "[He] was

one of God's ugliest creatures. He smelled bad, he looked bad... disgusting guy," Bailey grimaces. Sometimes a bit of ruckus broke loose once all the kids were seated. "For a nickel you could buy a roll of Necco wafers," Bailey recounts. "People would sit in the back and unwrap that whole row. Then at some point you'd *throw* it, and all this flickers through all the lights and scatters over everybody." After the movie, he and his friends crossed the street to the drugstore for a milkshake or a soda. The costly 30 cent banana splits were reserved only for days when you really wanted to show off. "That was a great Saturday. That's what life was all about," Bailey says.

In the early fifties Rose Klimek was an older

high school student. In her three years working at the Lamar, she most clearly remembers the weekend *Gone with the Wind* returned to the big screen. "The owner of the Lamar Theater was a big fan of the movie and he got a good deal. I think it cost a whopping 50 cents to see it," she recalls. "I had to listen to the dialogue so many times while selling popcorn that I could almost repeat it word for word." Klimek fondly recalls the innocent courting that went on between teenagers in the neighborhood, especially at the movies on Friday or Saturday nights. "I broke up with one boy at the theater before the movie started and sat with another one during the movie," she says. This boy shouldn't be pitied too much, since he later, "returned holding hands with another girl." Young couples proclaimed these short-lived relationships by etching their initials inside hearts on wooden booths at Mr. Luck's Hamburgers a few doors down from the theater.

Connie Knight remembers when she went to a movie at the Lamar in the sixties and the screaming was so loud, she could not even hear the film. It was not a horror flick; rather, Beatle mania caused such strong reactions. "What I remember most is going to see *A Hard Day's Night* with four girlfriends. I was eleven. We sat on the front row and everyone was screaming like the Beatles were really there," Knight recalls. Not until thirty years later, when she watched the movie on VHS, did she actually hear any of it. Knight remembers the strong smell of popcorn that wafted between the heavy velvet curtains. "I saw a lot of movies there during those years. Every Elvis movie released. We went every Saturday during the summer months.

It was always a fun time I looked forward to each weekend." Knight was able to see all these movies for just 50 cents – a price that included both admission and concessions.

The Lamar Theater closed in the 1960s, but reopened a decade later as a completely different type of movie theater. Gone were the days of rowdy school kids harmlessly throwing candy around on a Saturday afternoon. Instead, men surreptitiously walked up to the ticket window and snuck inside for pornographic films.

A poster outside Lamar Theater during its days as an adult theater. **Courtesy of Stoy Bailey.**

Memphis became a sort of "hub" for the adult film industry. These productions combined with Memphis' genteel Southern culture, made it a choice location for a federal obscenity trial. In 1972, the theater played a preview for *Deep Throat*, the "most famous X-rated movie of them all." The star of the film, Harry Reems, among others associated with it, was convicted of conspiring to distribute pornography in the most expensive federal trial in Memphis history. The conviction was later overturned in 1977 when obscenity laws changed.

This particular screening did more than spark a landmark lawsuit. It also played a part in an urban legend that has persisted decades later. *Deep Throat* was reportedly funded by the mafia and rumor has it a few Mafioso paid a visit to the theater. At the end of the show, "film "distributors" came by the ticket office to collect their share of the day's sales. Management refused to pay them anything. Later that night the theater caught fire. However, no evidence or personal account of this fire has ever surfaced.

Regardless of lawsuits, the theater continued to play adult films well after Reems and the lawyers left town. A grown up Stoy Bailey – now a community organizer who works in his historic neighborhood – often sauntered up to the theater with his camera, usually sans film, to "photograph" the clientele. He laughingly recalls how quickly they turned around and walked the other way as soon as they saw him standing there with a camera. Sometimes the lady who ran the ticket booth caught him snapping pictures of the customers or of the ads on the wall and would chase him away with a gun.

Bailey and others finally succeeded in shutting down the Lamar. Now they hope to give it a new life. "We're not trying to re-create the neighborhood of the past; that's done and gone," Bailey insists, "but we are trying to have a very strong say-so in the neighborhood of the future." They hope to see the Lamar Theater create memories for neighborhood children once again, this time as a performing arts center.

Painting of Walker Radiator Works sign. **Rebecca Phillips.**

STREET RODDING WITH WALKER RADIATOR WORKS

In the 1970s, Randy Clark and his brother searched for a 1941 Ford pickup truck just like the one their dad drove from 1950 to 1970. "It was red with yellow wheels and could get up to 90 mph in second gear. It had a 'hot rod' flathead and it was Dad's truck, and if it at all possible I would ride 'shot gun,'" Clark wrote about the vehicle that inspired his love for cars. When his father was diagnosed with cancer, he suddenly expressed a desire to drive his old 1941 pickup again. Clark continued, "My dad had never asked or even hinted that he wished to have his old '41 running again. I called up my brother and we quickly hatched a plan to find a '41 pickup…" They finally found one in California and restored it as a Christmas gift for their dad. A Walker radiator kept the pickup running for the last fifty years.

Harry Walker founded Walker Radiator Works in 1932. "We were just a radiator repair shop," says the founder's son, Vernon Walker, "and then it got to be we were the Mid-South's largest radiator repair shop." Harry Walker had only a third grade education, but that did not keep him from creating a thriving family business. Vernon stresses how hard his parents worked, "Back then they would work fifteen to eighteen hours in the day." He remembers working many nights and every Saturday, especially in the spring and summer, when most people had radiator problems. He started working at the shop full time in 1958, after he graduated from Frayser High.

Since the shop was next door to Sun Studio, they had interesting run-ins with the musical talent going to and fro. Harry Walker often ran Elvis and others off because they parked in front of the garage and blocked the way for repair jobs. One day Walker was across the street eating at Miss Taylor's restaurant, when his brother-in-law, who worked at Sun Studio, came looking for him. Jerry Lee Lewis' drummer was ill, so his band needed a fill-in. Walker played a session with the group, but called it quits before he played any gigs with them. "Back then they were just hitting beer joints and all because that's where their music was hot at, so I just didn't do it," Vernon recalls. After Sun Studio closed, he went in and explored the empty building. "They had left just stacks and stacks of 45 records," he recalls in amazement, "over in the corner, scattered on the floor… they were everywhere." He and his buddies discovered the records would fly a very satisfying distance when flung from a car. "We probably threw away a fortune! Back then, though, it was just junk."

It should come as no surprise that the owner of a radiator repair shop would be a car guy. Harry Walker was a particular fan of antique cars, especially T-Models, all of which his son Vernon now owns. The collection holds a 1906 N-Model Ford, a 1910 Cadillac touring car, a 1910 white Model T Roadster, and a very rare 1919 Essex touring car that once belonged to Pancho Villa. It took two weeks for Walker to add the Essex to his collection. He purchased it across the border, south of Mexico City, for fifty-two dollars. Harry Walker and his wife would even take road trips in an antique car. "Him and Mama got in the Roadster and drove it to Denver, and that was back in the fifites. He didn't care, he was having fun!" Walker says, remembering his father's love for cars.

Around 1959, Walker Radiator expanded into custom-made radiators for cars, buses, and industrial equipment, some dating back to 1886. The company installed new equipment and hired seven trained specialists who could each build an entire radiator by himself. The new factory line could replicate a factory model or complete special orders in four hours, which allowed the shop to offer "one-day drive-in service." Small radiator shops throughout the Mid-South also placed special orders with Walker Radiator so they could keep less inventory in their shops.

When Harry Walker passed away in 1966, three of his children took up the family business. Nieces and nephews later followed suit. By 1969, Walker Radiator was far more than just a repair business. They made radiators for street rods, but soon ended the repair business altogether in favor of manufacturing. Most modern radiators are made with aluminum, but Walker Radiator went against the grain and became one of the few companies to manufacture radiators with longer lasting copper and brass. "We probably manufacture four or five hundred different models," Walker estimates. They do everything, from building each and every piece of the radiator, to product packaging.

Vernon Walker and other enthusiasts formed the National Street Rod Association in 1970. They participate in eleven street rod events a year, starting around April. Walker brings two 1939 Chevrolet two-door sedans to the events, one green and one blue. He uses one of the cars for east coast events, and the other for the west

coast. "I drive to all of them. This one car I've got has 144,000 miles on it… I enjoy driving the car," he says. The association has grown to 54 thousand members and publishes a monthly magazine. Their largest event spans four days in Louisville, Kentucky. Ten to twelve thousand cars arrive there, eighty percent of them with Walker radiators.

Part of the radiators' testing process involved Walker's own blue and green street rods. "When we were doing an event in Sacramento, California, I'd always… go up to Death Valley and I'd spend a day in there in my car, just testing the performance of the radiator." His methods are simple. "When you get in temperatures of 125 degrees outside and you can… get out of it and leave the air conditioner running and walk back later and it's still sitting there, normal, you've got a winner." They ran this test each year, always trying to improve the radiator's performance and strength.

The first street rod Vernon Walker built himself was a 1926 Ford Model T sedan, which is still parked at his house. The first car he ever bought, a brand new 1957 Chevrolet Bel-Air, keeps the sedan company. He remembers how he earned the $2,435 to purchase the car. "We lived out on a farm out in Frayser… I had 24 head of white-faced cattle; I sold those. And then I had one hundred acres of soybeans; I sold it all," Walker says. He then told his dad he wanted to buy a new car. "Of course, I was 16 years old. Back then you couldn't own a car. So it was in Daddy's name." Walker kept it after all this time and had it restored about ten years ago.

In addition to a love for old cars, Walker also appreciates old signs. His extensive sign collection began with one that stood just down the street from Walker Radiator. Weakly Equipment Company was the Mid-South's largest lawn mower repair shop. The sign for this family business made quite an impression on him. "It's a man pushing an old, real lawn mower. He's walking, and the wheel turns and grass is popping out of it," Walker says, describing how the neon lights created the illusion of movement. "Everyone was always talking about that sign." Eventually, Weakley

moved to a new location across the street, but the sign was too big to take with them. Walker walked down, asked to buy it, and took it home shortly thereafter. "I knew if I hadn't gotten that sign it'd end up in scrap. That's where most signs do end up," he says. He currently has 477 signs in his collection.

His own business sign was installed around 1952. It measures eleven feet tall and features a fascinating display of moving lights that creates a "dripping" radiator effect. Because it is

Custom-built clone of a 1941 pickup truck owned by Randy Clark's father.
Courtesy of Hot Rods & Custom Stuff

A look at the Walker radiator that has been inside the truck for over fifty years.
Courtesy of Hot Rods & Custom Stuff

a painted sign rather than porcelain, it has to be retouched every five to six years. The dripping radiator sign's removal from the building is no small task. Since city laws now prohibit signs hanging over the sidewalk, Walker had to complete special paperwork to keep the sign's grandfathered status. "When we took it down, you're talking about people coming down!" Walker says, laughing. As they removed the sign for repairs, an astonished crowd gathered and shouted up at them, anxious to know if they were either going out of business or getting rid of the sign. One man demanded to know if the drip was still going to work when the sign was put back up.

Sometimes tourists stop to photograph the Walker Radiator sign. "I had a guy this morning, when I was coming in, trying to take a picture of the sign. It was still kind of dark… and I went and turned the lights on. You'd think I'd given him a million dollars," Walker says. Others, there for a tour of Sun Studio, detour to Walker instead when they recognize the company from street rodding. "If they're car people… we'll walk them through," he says, proud of both his antique sign and the business it represents.

"FOR A FEW YEARS IT WAS COVERED UP AND IT WASN'T LOVE'S FEED ANYMORE."

— JESSICA LOVE

Painting of Love's Feed ad on the east side of Peerless Printing. The wall was recently painted over. **Rebecca Phillips.**

A CITY'S LOVE FOR LOVE'S FEED

Welder and doghouse builder Billy Love was restless. Ready to do something different, he was drawn to the idea of opening his own business. Together with his father, they considered what kind of company to start. They first considered a doghouse factory, but eventually embarked on a feed store. In October 1988, Love's Feed Store opened on the corner of Cooper Street and Central Avenue.

Love only had a few thousand dollars to invest in the store's beginning stages. He didn't even have enough funds to place wholesale supply orders. "It was pretty tight when we first opened," he recalls. They couldn't afford a telephone or heat for the first six months. "There used to be a phone booth down on the corner. I had to go down there to use the phone," he says. Embarrassingly, a business across the street received calls from Love's customers, asking about prices and such. For the first three years he worked every day of the week, and twelve hour days at that.

Love felt the location near the Cooper-Young neighborhood was ideal for his business. "There are a lot of animal lovers there in Midtown," says Love. Undoubtedly, a shop that sold everything from pet food to live fowl, like peacocks and chickens, was an important one. He appreciated the "artsy" atmosphere and hosted exhibits during community art events. Love kept a close eye on his customers' needs, which created a loyal following. He cultivated relationships with customers that chose Love's Feed, even if they lived closer to the competition. "Hollywood Feed was probably one of my biggest competitors back then. They'd been around probably fifty years and I was putting a bite on their business," Love recalls, laughing, "I guess they were kind of shocked... everybody was I guess."

Love's Feed was known for fun traditions like the annual Halloween straw man. "That was kind of my invention," Love explains. Each year he took bales of hay stacked high on a storage unit and shaped them into a gigantic, seated straw man. "Every year they would take a picture of it for *The Commercial Appeal*," Love laughs at the memory of how a new photographer thought he was getting a scoop each October. "It actually started at the Zoo Boo. I sold a lot of feed to the zoo... and I sold them the straw. They wanted me to do something to attract attention so I thought of that," Love says, "then I put it at the store to attract attention to the store!" The straw men still live on, only now at Love's home instead of in Midtown.

The large Love's Feed warehouse mural on Walnut Grove Road was another way to catch the eyes of Memphians. The ad was painted in the mid-nineties by the same sign painter who put "Love's Feed" above the Midtown store's door. "We basically just did it as an attention grabber," Love says. The Science Diet dog food company paid for at least half of the ad, if not all of it.

Photographer Jeremy Greene noticed the mural flash by his truck window each time he passed it. Greene recalls, "I drove an old truck – a 1966 Chevy C20 Custom Camper Special. I particularly enjoyed driving well over the speed limit down the hill and around the curve as Walnut Grove merged into Union Avenue under the Poplar bridge. I would drive that way often and see the old building painted with the words 'Love Science' on it. It was covered in weeds and bushes so I never knew exactly what it said." Greene revisited the spot when he started Memphis Type and explains his experience, "I began to go out of my way to see and photograph signs, walls, graffiti and such. And so I stopped one day and parked and walked over to get a closer look. It actually said 'Love's Feed Science Diet' on the entire wall. I had an iPhone and an Olio Clip wide angle lens with me, so that's what I took a picture with that day." Although Love's Feed only used the warehouse for a couple of years, the red and white painted ad remained on the exterior wall for nearly two decades.

Love's unique experience with animals, particularly fowl, brought him a bit of attention from film crews in the Memphis area. Love made his own silver screen début in the 1992 movie, *Where the Red Fern Grows II*. A Love's Feed customer associated with the film struck a deal with him – Love could appear in the film in exchange for using his Redbone Coonhounds in the movie. "I had a speaking part but he cut it out," Love laughs, "I had to say it several times and I thought they were going to put it in the movie for as much time as they spent on it." Love's involvement in the film had him listed in the Memphis Blue Book as an "animal wrangler." On past Christmases, Love took his birds and animals to private parties in Graceland's stable, and even once spotted Lisa Marie Presley there. He still gets called to wrangle chickens and other fowl on set, which is how he began work on his most recent gig, a Trace Adkins music video.

Some of Love's brushes with fame were less exciting than others. He once made four large doghouses for Jerry Lee Lewis. As he pulled up to Lewis' house outside of Nesbit, Mississippi,

Love's Feed Store, formerly at the intersection Cooper Street and Central Avenue. **Courtesy of Billy Love.**

about twenty dogs of all shapes and sizes came barking down the drive. Love recalls, "He never did come out. He handed me an autograph through the door." Love safely stored the autograph in a scrapbook that documents his years running the store.

Rufus Thomas, who recorded at both Sun Studio and Stax Records, came in with his wife to select a Christmas tree. "He just walked all around the lot with his hands behind his back... His wife was actually shopping," Love recalls. After confirming he was indeed the legendary singer, Love requested an autograph. "Five dollars," Thomas replied. Love decided to pass. At the end of the shopping trip, however, Love says, "He ended up giving me one."

When illusionist David Copperfield performed at the Coliseum (around 2001), his team acquired chickens from Love. Thinking back on what Copperfield planned for the chickens makes Love and his daughter, Jessica Love, laugh. "They were going to do a magic trick with them... make a chicken disappear or something," they say nearly at the same time. Regardless of what tricks were in store for the fowl, Love grew his collection with yet another autograph. A scribbled note from Memphis' legendary Prince Mongo rounds out this collection. Prince Mongo regularly came to the store without shoes on, to buy rat poison. The note is addressed to "Spirit Billy," and thanks Love for the rat poison. "We want to be ready to get the demons," Prince Mongo wrote before he signed his name.

Daughter, Jessica, and her younger brother, Matt, grew up in the Love's Feed store. "I made a little crib right behind the desk," Love

remembers. The two kids constantly explored and played in what they believed was one of the biggest places around. "We had those big semi-trailers where we'd store stuff. So we'd run and hide and play on those... I remember thinking how big it was. Because when you're little everything is so big," Jessica says, laughing at how huge the store seemed to her as a kid. She recalls how proud she felt when she ran the cash register and sold "dog biscuits for a nickel," just like the grownups.

Love's son Matt got his first busking experience playing saxophone in front of the

Jessica Love in front of her dad's store.
Courtesy of Billy Love.

store. Once, *The Commercial Appeal* came by and snapped a photo of his performance. "He got tips every once in a while," Love recalls. His kids' other business ventures included vegetable and lemonade stands at Love's shop. Jessica laughs, "We thought we were so fancy and rich getting a quarter and stuff."

As a single father with two kids, Love felt he could not sustain the seven-day-a-week business. "My two kids were more important to me," he says. He closed Love's Feed Store in 2008, which made way for Midtown Nursery to hold the corner for a few years. In 2013, an innovative food truck restaurant, the Truck Stop, was approved for the site. As they prepared to move, the nursery's owners took down their sign from the storefront and revealed the hand-painted Love's Feed sign underneath. For a few short weeks, its brilliant black letters shined on bright white paint once again. "For a few years it was covered up and it wasn't Love's Feed anymore," Jessica says, thinking back, "but then when they started tearing it down again, that [nursery] went away. So it got torn down as Love's Feed." For those few weeks, she could drive by that corner and reminisce about the childhood she enjoyed there.

Peerless Printing is the latest business to occupy what was once the Love's Feed warehouse. The printing company passed through four families since it began in 1928 and currently includes the Freys, who purchased the business in 2013. The building houses multiple printing presses and other machinery that supports the commercial printing business. As soon as the Freys obtained the business, they began cleaning and fixing up the building. Unfortunately, the exterior walls were fairly deteriorated, in desperate need of a power wash and new paint. Alas, the Love's Feed Science Diet advertisement was painted over. "I would've loved for it to have been kept. I like those kinds of things," owner Jennifer Frey says wistfully. Her husband, Brant agrees, "I always did love that… it was a neat sign."

Most, if not all, of the signs that prove Love's Feed ever existed are gone from the streets of Memphis. The small store was demolished and the advertisement on the warehouse painted over. However, Jessica still finds connections to the past. "My best friend, who I didn't meet until I was ten, her parents used to come there when we were babies. We probably passed each other not even knowing it," Jessica says, "I go to Christian Brothers [University] now and my advisor, she used to… go and buy her dog food there. She was just telling me, 'you know they closed down Love's Feed.' Didn't even know I had a connection to it… It's funny how many people in Memphis know of that place or have heard of it… and the connections you get between that," Jessica says with a smile.

Painting of the rusty Normal Beauty Shop sign. This is the last remaining sign that makes reference to Normal Station, an older name for the district. **Rebecca Phillips.**

A VERY NORMAL LIFE AT THE NORMAL BEAUTY SHOP

The unassuming sign leans precariously over the sidewalk. The rusted letters advertise a place that no longer exists. Calling its phone number will not help one get a new hairdo. A person might be confused as to why the sign next to an alterations shop is still there at all. In fact, this sign is the last physical reminder of a neighborhood once called Normal Station. The neighborhood began quite normally and lived up to its conventional name. The community grew by means of a "normal" school, and filled up with residents who calmly went about their very normal business, day in and day out.

The earliest records of the area date back to 1823 when Revolutionary War veterans, Tyree Rhodes and William Dillon, were granted that tract of land. The property was later sold by their heirs for $2,062.50 to William F. Eckles. The railroad tracks came in 1835 as part of the region's first set rail line, and would later become the first railroad line in the country to connect the Atlantic Ocean with the Mississippi River in 1857. At that time a Native American hunting camp was still located on the Black Bayou, near Park Avenue. This strip of land was simply referred to as Eckles tract until the turn of the twentieth century. The city of Memphis would continue to grow eastward along these railroad tracks.

In 1909, Memphis leaped into the competition for one of four new "normal" state schools, or, teacher training colleges. Preparations for the new school began as soon as the city learned it won. Streets and streetcar tracks were laid in 1911, and construction began on the West Tennessee State Normal School. The first 200 students started classes in 1912. Aside from a two dollar registration fee, the college was free for Tennessee residents. The neighborhood and the college would walk lockstep through the rest of history.

The railroad and the streetcar system served the area's students and residents. A Craftsman-style train station called Normal Depot was built in front of the school. The streetcars offered five cent rides to the center of downtown, a seven mile trip that took forty minutes. The neighborhood called Normal Station was approximately one square mile inside the boundaries of Park Avenue on the south, Southern on the north, Highland on the west, and Goodlett on the east.

Commerce expanded as the neighborhood grew in the 1920s. Before long, anything a community might need in the form of grocery stores, a post office, and other places, were constructed. McLaurine's Bakery was the first to offer meals in the neighborhood. The bakery delighted neighborhood children like Pauline Caldwell well into the 1940s and 1950s. She recalls her favorite memories of the neighborhood and is quick to talk about the little bakery, "I can remember on Sunday going down there after church... we'd get a chocolate éclair for a nickel, which was fun." In 1925 the college's education program changed to a four year degree, which prompted a name change to State Teacher's College in Memphis. A neighborhood movie theater, officially named the Newman but known as the Normal, opened up on Highland in 1928. In keeping with theaters at the time, it served up memorable concessions and double features for kids on Saturdays.

Memphis annexed the little "town" of Normal Station in 1929. Automobile usage spread and altered the landscape of the area by 1949. The same year, the streetcar tracks were removed and one year later the train station was demolished. In 1957 the college was renamed as Memphis State University. The university expanded and

appropriated more land. Academic and athletic buildings, parking lots, and student housing increased the university's area.

Student presence in the neighborhood brought issues of segregation and civil rights to the forefront in the early sixties. While more well-known sit-ins and protests took place downtown or in the city's libraries, Normal Station made a few headlines when students demanded integration at a small restaurant on Highland. Eating areas in downtown stores were integrated in 1962, and other

Students protesting at the Normal Tea Shop in 1964. **Special Collections, University of Memphis Libraries, photo by Sandy Felsenthal.**

public areas followed suit in 1963. The Civil Rights Act of 1964 desegregated hotels and restaurants. In May 1964, six Memphis State students took a stand and staged a sit-in at the Normal Tea Room. A few days of picketing by more students followed the demonstration. Finally, in July the restaurant began to serve all students and people, regardless of color. The only tensions between the university and the neighborhood in recent years have been over school-owned rental properties and fraternities. For the most part Normal Station and the university exist in harmony.

Like everything else about Normal Station, its inhabitants' memories are all pretty, well... normal. Shirley Bell worked at Normal Beauty Shop for a few years after she attended beauty school, but back then, the establishment was called Marie's Beauty Shop. She remembers being frustrated with her career at first because it took a while to build up a clientele. Pauline Caldwell's mother would occasionally get her hair done at the same beauty shop for the most practical reasons. "Mother had naturally curly hair. The only time she went to the beauty shop was to get it cut," Caldwell says. Margie Hill grew up near the Highland Strip and started getting her hair done at the Normal Beauty Shop when her usual shop south of Park Avenue closed. "I only went for haircuts but my mom went every week. My hairstyle back then was called a bouffant and my mom's was kept permed and short," remembers Hill. Eventually, she was too hip for the shop's styling and changed up her 'do. "I grew it out and flipped up the ends, 'ratted' the top and cut some bangs," she says.

Caldwell was raised in Normal Station. "As a child, of course, I went to Essex School, which at that time was under twelve. It's no longer there. We'd walk half a block to school... It was a good place to be," she recalls, praising the good teachers she had. Even when school was out for the summer there was plenty to do right there in the neighborhood. "In the summertime we spent most of our time at the park. At that time there was a wading pool," she remembers. The Park Commission provided organized programs and games at the park. She recollects those summers, "In the afternoon when it got hot the girls would go sit in the shade and do crafts. I don't know what the boys did. That was the way we spent our summer. We didn't stay inside!"

The neighborhood was often described as quiet but bustling. "Except for the trains," Caldwell interjects. Many walked down to the Normal Theater for a movie. "I always went to that on Saturday. Sometimes I'd stay all day," Caldwell laughs as if shocked by her younger self. "At that time it cost twelve cents. And then it was 35 cents... I was tall for my age. I got tired of them asking how old I was so I just started paying the 35 cents." Tom Harder recalls afternoons spent at the theater in the 1950s with his younger brother, "We would see a serial, a cartoon and a double feature, either cowboys or monsters or a combination of both. After the movie we would leave by the side exits and be given a large can of Hi-C© orange juice." Margie Hill also frequented the little movie theater until it underwent some changes. "The Normal was changed to the Studio Theater in the late sixties which showed foreign films and what was called art films, which meant they were mostly adults only," she recalls.

Normal Station was a place where people lived quiet lives and made meaningful little memories. People were kind, even the deejays with big shot jobs, playing tunes on the radio. Hill tells of the time in the mid-sixties when she stood outside a peephole-like window and held up a little sign scrawled with a song request, "I remember when my two friends and I walked down Highland to WHBQ and peeked in the little window there where the DJ always sat. We held up a card asking him to play a song for us. I'm sure our song request was a Beatles song... We must have had a transistor radio with us because he did play our request and he dedicated it to the three girls looking in the window – Margie, Donna and Margaret!" While the little neighborhood has grown to be yet another part of Memphis, many out there still pass under the Normal Beauty Shop sign and think to themselves, I knew Normal.

"WHERE I GREW UP, IF I WENT OUT THE BACK GATE I WAS IN LEAHY'S TRAILER COURT... ITINERANT-TYPE PEOPLE WERE ALWAYS PASSING THROUGH. THERE WERE CARNIVAL PEOPLE, TOO. AND THERE WAS A LOT OF MUSIC." — CHARLIE MUSSELWHITE

Painting of Leahy's Trailer Park entrance sign. This arrow sign has been removed, though the park still rents homes to short-term and life-long residents. **Rebecca Phillips.**

LIVING THE GOOD LIFE AT LEAHY'S

Children on bikes pour out from a road that fades back into thick shade and tangled streets. Gangs of kids weave in and out of double wide trailers. They jet toward the front lawn where a pool used to be. Churches visit in the summertime to play soccer and other games with these younger residents. This is Leahy's Trailer Park and Weekly Rentals, one of the oldest establishments on Summer Avenue. Leahy's is the kind of place where a handful of people sit inside the main office and shoot the breeze even though a "closed" sign hangs on the door. A place like Leahy's, with humble campsite beginnings in the early 1900s, has a history steeped in both fact and rumor. Details of what may or may not have happened long ago are intertwined in the residents' collective memory.

Anna Scott is a California native and the ex-wife of Leahy's current owner, John Leahy. She and her daughter seem to run the business and clearly love how the stories about Leahy's are as much rumor as they are fact. Certainly, it is true that a beautiful, historic three-story home once stood at the front of the park. What may not be true is that "Machine Gun" Kelly, arrested in Memphis in 1933, frequented the house back when it (allegedly) operated as a bordello. Al Capone supposedly enjoyed the house, well before the Leahys owned it, of course.

Leahy's Motor Inn and Trailer Court opened in 1941. Arthur T. "Pop" and Edna Leahy inhabited an apartment in the home that once stood at the front of the park. Travelers enjoyed hot meals and maid service during their stay at the "Big House" until it closed in 1960. The Bryant twins lived at Leahy's for a number of years and remembered how Pop cared for everyone there. "Pop was like a daddy to everybody out here," one sister recalled. "He called this his little village, and he rode around it every night, stopping to check on people, to talk and see how everybody was doing."

When she was twelve JoAnne Jensen moved with her family from Illinois to Leahy's in the mid-forties. A self-described tomboy, scolded by Mrs. Leahy for playing football, Jensen was right in the thick of whatever the kids did at Leahy's. One of her earliest memories of Mr. Leahy was the time she and the neighborhood kids tried to build a playground. "We had no playground. So we went to the back part of the property and cleared it. By the time we got it cleared and the bases all laid out, Mr. Leahy came down, put in a telephone pole and lights, and parked trailers there. Our playground was gone again," she concludes, still feeling the sting of that injustice.

Although she never got the playground she worked so hard for, Jensen was the first person to swim in the Leahy's pool. The month was November, but she says she would not be deterred by something as trivial as the temperature, "I talked to Mr. Leahy, and he said I could. When they got it finished they let me know and I went over and got in!" She stayed in the freezing water, alone of course, for five or ten minutes. "It was cold!" she admits. "We were there so long that our kids could go swimming there," she adds.

Mrs. Jensen met her husband, George, at Leahy's when she was seventeen. They

Leahy's postcard featuring the pool out front and three story house no longer standing today. **Courtesy of Anna Scott.**

remember the first time they noticed each other before officially meeting. "She was up in a tree when I saw her," he laughs, recalling how much of a tomboy she was. "Our playground!" she quickly exclaims in her own defense. "We had to build a platform up in the tree and we strung a rope up there and we would jump off that platform onto that rope and swing. We played Tarzan," she laughs. The first time she saw him, he was headed to the bathhouse because the trailers had no inside bathrooms back then. "He would come up every morning, regular as clockwork. He'd have a roll of toilet paper under his arm, a swagger and a whistle, and he just was walking down the sidewalk there going to the bathhouse. That's when I first saw him," she says.

It took a little time for them to go on a date since she first thought he was interested in her friend. She and her girlfriend went riding with him in his mother's car. "Then finally he asked me to go out with him," Mrs. Jensen says.

"We got to where we went on Saturday. We'd go downtown, walk down Main Street..." They might get a snack at Walgreens, take a walk, or see a movie. Once married, the young couple got their own trailer at Leahy's, halfway between his and her parents.

The 1950s were truly Leahy's heyday. James Jones lived at Leahy's then, as he put the finishing touches on *From Here to Eternity*. The novel would go on to appear on Modern Library's list of "100 Best Novels," win the National Book Award for fiction, and inspire a film that won eight Academy Awards. Jones' friend Captain Patt Meara, another Leahy's resident in the fifties, recounted some of the goings-on there in that decade for *Memphis Magazine*, "One year during Cotton Carnival, Gypsy Rose Lee and her husband — I believe his name was Julio de Diego — lived in their trailer directly across the street from us. Oh yeah! And one of our neighbors was a contributing editor to *Encyclopedia Britannica.* Leahy's is definitely not the same."

Blues musician Charlie Musselwhite wrote about the influence of 1950s Memphis and Leahy's in the liner notes of his 2002 album, "One Night in America." Musselwhite describes a vibrant culture of travelers and music, "Where I grew up, if I went out the back gate I was in Leahy's Trailer Court... Itinerant-type people were always passing through. There were carnival people, too. And there was a lot of music." In

1947, Musselwhite moved to the house behind Leahy's on Manhattan Street, and stayed there until he left at eighteen in 1962.

His mother convinced Mr. Leahy to allow her to put a gate in the back fence so she could walk through the trailer court to get to the bus stop on Summer Avenue. A young Musslewhite had direct access to Leahy's and the many kids his age living there. "I had a lot of friends there and people would come and go because they were itinerant. Some of them

One of two remaining Leahy's Weekly Rentals signs on Summer Avenue, 2013.
Jeremy Greene.

were gypsies and some... were in the service, and some would get relocated there for work, or they were just looking for work. Nobody stayed forever. They kept moving along," he says of the transients he met there. One of Musselwhite's childhood friends was JoJo, the son of traveling entertainers. JoJo's father worked with the carnival and had a flat store (now more commonly known as a carnival game). "I would go to the fair and see him out there and sometimes he would let me play a round or two for free." Musselwhite also recalls JoJo's father bringing a helium tank home to blow up balloons for all the kids at Leahy's.

The stories of gypsies, musicians, writers, and others who drifted in and out of Leahy's, turned the place into a delightful pocket of Memphis history that still awaits any explorer willing to wander past the battered green sign. Like so many other Summer Avenue treasures, it almost faded away. When Pop passed away in 1971, management shifted to his children. Pop's son, Arthur F. Leahy, attempted to run the establishment from the West Coast, but the place did not stand up well to an absent owner.

By 1989, Leahy's was on the brink of demise. The mobile homes were gone and the cottages were about to be demolished. John Leahy, grandson of the founding Leahy, returned to Memphis to run the trailer park he loved since childhood. He was raised in Los Angeles and had only spent childhood summers at Leahy's. He left a swanky job as a celebrity limo driver in Beverly Hills, sought by the likes of

Muhammad Ali, to fix sewage issues and collect rent. Upon his return, he found many itinerant residents, just like the old days. For example, in 2005 most rentals belonged to steel workers who were in Memphis to build the FedEx Forum. However, others there had permanent homes in "Leahyville."

Betty Page from Dallas, Texas, is one of the oldest residents at Leahy's. At 85, she lives in a trailer with animal themed décor and a new backyard patio. She proudly shows pictures of this recent renovation on her iPhone. A resident since 1975, Page lived large in Memphis and wrote a book to tell about it. *I Got Ya Elvis, I Got Ya!* recounts her Elvis Presley-chasing exploits. According to Page, Elvis read the manuscript of her book and loved it. While most of her stories involve the King, Page is quick to share how safe she has felt living at Leahy's all these years.

While Mrs. Jensen speaks fondly of her years at Leahy's, a sort of wistfulness exists in her voice when she remembers how transitory it all felt. Residents came in and out of her life so quickly it was difficult to build lasting connections. "You'd meet people there and never see them again," she says. It is easy to imagine there are others around the country with fond memories of Leahy's. Perhaps some, like the Jensens, met and married because of the place. Maybe others made a friend they never forgot, though they surely lost touch. Even if the connections were lost, the memories never are.

"HE [BOBO THE CHIMP] COULD TAKE HIS FIST AND HIT IT ON THE FLOOR AND YOU COULD FEEL THE FLOOR MOVE." — JIMMY DAVENPORT

Painting of Skateland winged roller skate sign. Although the building caught fire, the sign remained intact. **Rebecca Phillips.**

ROLLER SKATE FOR HEALTH AT SKATELAND

Skateland on Summer Avenue is arguably the most beloved Memphis skating rink, known for both its wholesome history and its unique signage. Leo Pieraccini already owned a "swimming and dance hall complex" called Clearpool, when he opened Skateland in 1955. The original building housed one of the South's largest skating rinks. The iconic neon signage featured "SKATELAND" in large red letters, three roller skates with wings and rotating wheels, and the tagline "Roller Skate for Health."

Skaters rotated under a large wooden dome. On the wall above them, a neon signboard instructed them on what to do at any given moment. Activities included "All Skate," "Trios," "Reverse," and "Grand March." The "Skates Off" command signaled the end of their time on the rink. In 1958 the Southern Regional Roller Skating Championship was held at the rink.

After a little over a year operating Skateland, Pieraccini added a "family cabana swim club" to his Summer Avenue expansion plans. The Riveria was to be built beside the skating rink. Had it been built, Memphis families would have enjoyed swimming, tennis, badminton, shuffleboard, a playground, and a snack bar for a monthly price of one hundred dollars per family. Plans included fifty private, lockable cabanas, complete with a shower that would serve as dressing rooms for the most demure families.

The proposal seemingly never developed because in 1963, Skateland moved to a smaller location on Old Summer Avenue, essentially across the street. The original location's rink required only ten laps per mile whereas the

new, smaller rink required sixteen. The red neon letters, winged skates, and instructional signboard also traveled across the street. Various stores moved in and out of the original building throughout the years. Eventually the massive architectural windows were lost; today they are covered up by concrete panels.

In 1937, a group of roller rink owners formed the Roller Skating Rink Operators Association (RSROA, later changed to RSA). The RSROA promoted skating as a healthy pastime. Their policies created a positive, family-oriented identity for skating, and established best practices for rink operators. Skating gained momentum with the general public during the 1940s.

Until the 1970s, skates had wooden wheels that required white chalk powder to glide. Rinks were therefore covered in powder, which left skaters, "looking as if they'd come from a flower mill after a night at the rink." Skating became easier and safer with the proliferation of plastic wheels and coating for rinks. Many rinks added modern lights and music.

Disco roller skating fueled a huge spike in roller skating popularity throughout the seventies and eighties, although at the displeasure of the RSA. A 1987 article cites Susan Theis, senior editor of the organization's magazine, as saying, "We don't want to look like we're part of something that's going down the chute... We're geared to a family atmosphere that stresses discipline and security." This sentiment echoed the thoughts of at least one Memphis rink owner, Ted Moyes. His East End Skating Rink represented a new breed of rinks that stressed cleanliness and sophistication – not cheap entertainment.

Skateland closed its doors after a two-alarm fire in 2006, forty years after it opened. Over 100 firefighters fought the blaze while the community watched in sadness and disbelief. One onlooker, Terry Lebo, said at the scene, "I met my wife there. This is an incredibly sad night." Even the division fire chief spoke as he watched the building be consumed with black smoke, "This is hard because I've skated here, and this place, like a lot of Memphis landmarks, holds a lot of memories for a lot of people."

Jimmy Davenport worked at Skateland for eleven years. One of his most memorable moments at the rink was when he taught a chimpanzee how to roller skate. When a couple came in one day and asked if he and his

The original Skateland building before the business moved to Old Summer Road. **Special Collections, University of Memphis Libraries.**

A postcard of the Skateland interior. The floors were made of maple. **Memphis and Shelby County Room, Memphis Public Library & Information Center.**

coworkers would teach the chimp to skate, they immediately agreed. "Of course we said yes, not knowing what we were getting into," Davenport recalls, "You would not believe how strong he was. He could take his fist and hit it on the floor and you could feel the floor move."

They pulled Bobo the chimp with ropes to teach him how to skate. When Bobo completed his lessons, his owners often brought him to skate with the public during regular sessions. Apparently Bobo also performed at Libertyland. Davenport is not alone in his fond memories of the sock hops and private parties he enjoyed at Skateland with a group he remains friends with to this day. Across the country, many are likely to have similar accounts of their own local skating rinks.

While the doors to the skating rink closed after the fire, the signage was undamaged and remained atop the building to usher in a new era of occupants. County Glass and Glazing, LLC took over the Skateland building in 2007. They left the iconic signs above the building and the neon signboard is still displayed on the wall inside. The company kept the large skate above the building. "He wanted to keep the skate so people could see where he was. He'll say 'come to the skate,'" explains Darla Dunn and David Moyes. The skating rink itself took on a new life under the hands of Caleb Sweazy. Sweazy moved to Memphis after Skateland closed, so he never experienced the skating rink. A love for salvaged materials, rather than nostalgia, drove his involvement in the next stage of Skateland's history.

Sweazy answered County Glass' ad to purchase the skating rink flooring. "I like to find interesting materials and reuse things, especially when they have some sort of historical significance," Sweazy explains, "They were kind of gutting the building. So they had taken the flooring and sawed it up into these big sheets and just stacked them up." Sweazy launched Firebrand Furniture and got to work. He turned the four by eight foot sheets of maple into roughly ten custom furniture pieces to fill special requests for roller derby girls and Skateland regulars who wanted a piece of Memphis history. He also sold some pieces at the Cooper Young Festival that year, "with a toddler in one hand and a guitar in the other."

Passersby can still enjoy a small part of this well-loved Memphis landmark as they drive down Summer Avenue or Sam Cooper Boulevard. Many stop at the glass company parking lot to snap their own photographs of the Skateland sign and the can't-miss-it winged skate.

The Skateland legacy lives on at Skateland Raleigh for everyone who wants to don a pair of roller skates. This rink shares a name and a partnership with the Skateland on Summer Avenue that Pieraccini opened in 1973. Ted Moyes taught skating at two of Pieraccini's rinks in prior years, and opened a Frayser skating rink with him about ten years earlier. Now Moyes' daughter, Trisha Hall, and his grandchildren are partners in this rink, as well as in the others Moyes later opened. They reminisce about the days of skating competitions and national champions that came through those rinks. "We had speed, figure, dance, art, and believe it or not... instead of pairs it was called fours. They would skate and do all these tricks... It was amazing," his

daughter and granddaughter recount almost simultaneously.

Cameron Gunn first visited Skateland Raleigh at thirteen. He became an excellent skater and eventually started to work there. He returned to work at his favorite hangout during breaks even after he left for college. He came back permanently soon after his education ended. "My heart's in music, so if I could I'd probably spin records all day," Gunn

*Trish Moyes and Pete McCrory at a competition in Florida, 1954. Skateland employees trained many skillful roller skating competitors. **Courtesy of Raleigh Skateland.***

Skateland sign atop County Glass and Glazing LLC, 2014. **Jeremy Greene.**

says of his deejay duties at the rink. "He can get them moving," Darla exclaims. Working as a disk jockey at a skating rink requires a love for the skating center, a fun-loving attitude, and knowledge of the different centers' musical preferences and routines. New deejays are trained by older deejays and managers and often stay on for many years.

Hartwell Strain is an example of the wholesome pastime that roller skating was and still is today. As a seventh grader, Strain had his first date at Skateland Raleigh. "Back then Skateland was the place to be on Friday nights," Strain recalls, "Only one problem is, I didn't

know how to skate. I wanted to make a good impression." Leading up to this grand event, his father dutifully took him to Skateland nearly every day after school for a week and half.

Thankfully, Strain was ready for his big night. He stipulates, "Now I wasn't turning any crazy corners or anything but I learned well enough to stay on my feet and be able to hold hands and dance around... they always had slow songs too that they played." Many Memphians likely have similar memories as Raleigh Skateland and other roller rinks in the city were prime locations for youthful date nights. Some even relive the glory days of the skating rink. A group that skated as children in the 1970s recently had a reunion at Raleigh Skateland.

No matter the age, individuals can still have a fun date night or wholesome family outing at any of the three rinks still run by the family of one of the Memphis' first skating rink founders. The business has changed drastically in the last year due to competition from other business models. "Anything in the skating center that you can't tangibly touch has now been changed," Dunn explains, "It's been a crazy year... new logos, new birthday parties, we're about to do emails to people who are interested in knowing what's going on with the skating center. Did we think that there were people out there who wanted that? No!" They all laugh, clearly excited about new marketing efforts and a realization that roller skating isn't just a thing of the past. "The kids grow up and then there are other children being born. And so there are parents always looking for fun ideas for their kids," they say.

Painting of the Lorraine Motel sign. The building was converted into The National Civil Rights Museum. **Rebecca Phillips.**

RISING UP FROM THE LORRAINE MOTEL

The building that would eventually become the Lorraine Motel was built around 1925. Originally called the Windsor Hotel, the structure was renamed the Marquette Hotel in 1945 and put up for sale. Walter Bailey, a former railroad porter, and his wife, Loree, bought the building. They moved from the rooming house they ran on Vance Avenue to their living quarters at the hotel. Inspired by the song, "Sweet Lorraine," and by his wife, Bailey renamed the hotel the Lorraine.

Because Bailey had prior experience working on the railroad, he knew that segregation made it difficult for his black clientele to find a place to eat and stay while traveling. His upscale hotel and restaurant served his famous barbecue, home-cooked meals, and welcomed both black and white guests. His apparent success allowed him to expand the hotel a couple of times. He added a second story and drive-up access to the rooms, necessitating a name change to the Lorraine Motel. At one point, he added a pool encircled by a six foot tall pierced brick fence.

The design of Bailey's Lorraine Motel bore a strong resemblance to the original Holiday Inn, considered the "epitome" of travel back then. "The whole motif of the Lorraine Motel, with the green doors and the big marquee and everything was modeled after the Holiday Inn motels," explains Barbara Andrews, Director of Education and Interpretation for the National Civil Rights Museum. The Holiday Inn styled marquee on the south side of the building and the neon signs for the motel and café on the north end were likely put in place in the late fifties. The horizontal Lorraine Motel sign on the south wall featured bright neon letters. The sign was completely repainted as part of the museum's renovations in 2013–2014.

"The Lorraine was really one of the top-notch hotels in terms of amenities, again borrowing after the Holiday Inn," Andrews continues. Outside, the establishment had convenient parking and a pool with a large patio around it. Once inside, guests enjoyed what were very nice rooms for the era. Each room was well appointed with nightstands, a coffee table, an adjoining private bath, and decorative drapes. "It was a bustling little place," concludes Andrews.

The Lorraine Motel and the Lorraine Café were two of the rare places where integration was the norm, especially for those in the entertainment industry where "the lines weren't so rigid about black and white." Recording artists with Stax Records were frequent guests, as black and white artists often collaborated and wrote songs there. While at the motel, musicians sometimes brought recording equipment and instruments and played long into the night. Many a hit song was written at the Lorraine in its heyday during the fifties and sixties. Bailey created a place where anyone could be, no matter their skin color; and yet, an act of racism would bring it to ruin.

On April 4, 1968, Dr. Martin Luther King, Jr., was assassinated on the balcony of Room 306 at the Lorraine Motel. The same day Bailey's wife had a brain hemorrhage and died five days later. "I didn't live here at the time, but from what people have said there was a cloud that kind of descended over the city... Having just experienced the garbage strike and having seen the trucks rolling in, and feelings just still being very raw, many people felt a lot of guilt about being here in the city where Dr. King was killed," says Andrews. The area around the Lorraine and south of downtown was virtually abandoned. The only buildings left were dilapidated shotgun houses, several warehouses, and an empty nightclub. The only open businesses, aside from the Lorraine, were a nearby lounge and the Arcade Restaurant. The motel's clientele shifted to prostitutes and a handful of permanent residents.

Lorraine Motel, April, 1973. That year saw motel residents evicted and homes demolished for the museum project. **Special Collections, University of Memphis Libraries.**

Bailey maintained rooms 306 and 307 as a memorial to both King and his wife. The only public reminder of King's death was a small shrine the Southern Christian Leadership Conference placed outside room 306, which consisted of a plaque and a glass enclosure around the door. Bailey added his late wife's shoes and books, and King's dishes from his last meal. Visitors could peer inside and see a few photographs of King by Ernest Withers on the walls. In 1982, the inevitable moment came – foreclosure.

The team that assembled to save the Lorraine had a difficult road ahead of them. First they had to get the Lorraine back. When the Lorraine Civil Rights Museum foundation did not raise enough money to pay the motel's mortgage, they found themselves on the steps of the Shelby County Courthouse on December 13, 1982, eager to purchase the building at auction. Upon arrival, they received a contribution from the Memphis sanitation workers' union. Armed with these additional funds, the foundation's representatives were able to stay in the game. The final course of action came down to two persons: D'Army Bailey, who bid for the foundation and Harry Sauer, who owned the motel's mortgage. At the last minute the Tri-State Bank offered a fifty thousand dollar loan if they could find an underwriter right then. Two underwriters were found at the courthouse so bidding ended with Bailey going a few thousand dollars over the final amount raised by the foundation. He signaled his limit to Sauer, who did not bid again.

The foundation settled on the idea to turn the site into a civil rights movement museum. Ben Lawless, retired exhibition director of the

Turning the Lorraine Motel into the National Civil Rights Museum. **Courtesy of Barbara Andrews.**

Smithsonian Institution's National Museum of American History, and consultant for Elvis Presley Enterprises' creation of Graceland tourism, came on board. The foundation eventually raised the 8.8 million dollars needed to turn the vision into reality, which was no easy task. By 1987, they had the funds and selected McKissack and McKissack, the black-owned Nashville architecture firm responsible for the Universal Life Insurance Company building, for the project.

On January 10, 1988, the Lorraine closed its doors as a motel. The next time it opened to the public it would be a museum. The motel's last resident, Jacqueline Smith, did not go willingly. She ignored the eviction notice and was eventually removed by law enforcement. "If I can't live at the Lorraine, I'll camp out on the sidewalk out front," she reportedly stated. Camp outside she did, and began her decades long protest against the museum. She once explained, "I think the reason for having a museum at the site of Dr. King's death for educational purposes

lacks substance because we have a run-down neighborhood, poverty, homelessness, crime, drug abuse, all these ills that plague our society." Smith opposed what she saw as gentrification of the area around the museum, and claimed the museum was just a tool to displace black people from the neighborhood.

On a joyous July 4, 1991, over five thousand people gathered for the museum's dedication ceremony. Rosa Parks cut the ribbon, stating, "When I came to Memphis to join the march along with Mrs. King [April 8, 1968], I could not even think about coming to this site. I did not want to see the place where he lost his life. But today I'm very happy and proud to be here and be part of this museum." Barbara Andrews walked through the museum for the first time that day. Only a few trucks and buses were inside – the rest of the "exhibits" were just artist renderings taped on the wall. "The walls were just back to the bare paneling with just these large drawings... so you could get a sense of what the space was going to look like," Andrews recalls. Just two months later, on September 28, 1991, upwards of 900 visitors came to the museum on its first official day. In protest of the museum, Jacqueline Smith played King's "I Have a Dream Speech" at full volume from across the street during the ceremonies.

Andrews has been at the museum many years now since her first walk through the near-empty building in 1991. The annual Freedom Awards has been one of the most memorable aspects of her time there. The Freedom Award "honors individuals who have made significant contributions in civil rights and who have laid the foundation for present and future leaders in the battle for human rights," while serving as "a symbol of the ongoing fight for human rights both in America and worldwide." A caveat for receiving the award is to provide the museum with an oral history. Andrews treasures the interviews she's conducted with these notable leaders. "You get to really dig into who they are and where they've come from. Many of them are so very candid and their beginnings

were just as humble or ordinary as anybody else's," says Andrews. "They saw a need, they were courageous, they decided to take a stand. They didn't start out to be leaders in it, they just started out to act."

Erica S. Qualy came to Memphis a few years ago to attend Memphis College of Art. Of all the things she has experienced in the city, the museum has made one of the strongest impressions. She usually plans to take her out-of-town guests to the museum to experience it firsthand. "It's kind of depressing to some people but I think it's really important to Memphis history," Qauly says. For her, the Lorraine Motel is so much more than just a building that houses memories. Instead, it reminds her to reflect on what the future of race relations in the U.S. should look like. "It's a really good place to soak it all in, how big the problem was and how it finally came to a head and is still going on... You realize the problem is still here, in Memphis and in other places as well," Qualy reflects.

The museum's 2013–2014 renovations

The National Civil Rights Museum during transformation from motel to museum. **Courtesy of Barbara Andrews.**

Over 5,000 people gathered for the museum's dedication ceremony on July 4, 1991.
Courtesy of Barbara Andrews.

broadened the scope of what was already an impactful experience. The original plan was to fix peeling wallpaper and restore yellowed photographs, but the plan changed to completely reconstruct the exhibits. The process began with museum staff who listed themes they thought lacked coverage in the exhibits. In late 2012 they formed a committee of leading historical scholars from all over the country. "That whole year it was like going to school," recalls Andrews. "We'd sit around the room... and they'd just talk to us about history." The museum gained a greater historical perspective because of this tedious, eighteen-month-long process of writing and revising the text that would go on the walls, the identification of people in photographs, and

other tasks that went into the renovation.

Walter Bailey passed away about nine years before the museum opened. He never saw the symbol of freedom and sacrifice his little motel became for the generations that followed him. To Andrews he is an example of how "everyday people can make a difference." He was one of the first to realize the site of Dr. King's death had historical significance and should be preserved, which in turn made today's National Civil Rights Museum possible as it stands today. She admires, "he really had the vision that this site should not just be bulldozed over or turned into a parking lot. He was, in many ways, sort of before his time."

"HE WAS RECORDING PEOPLE THAT NOBODY ELSE WOULD RECORD. HE DID IT INTENTIONALLY BECAUSE HE SAID RIGHT HERE IN MEMPHIS WAS AN ENTIRE RACE OF PEOPLE THAT WERE NOT GIVEN A CHANCE TO PROVE THEMSELVES."

— MEMPHIS JONES

Painting of Sam Phillips Recording sign on the building Phillips purchased in 1958.
Rebecca Phillips.

AFTER SUN STUDIO:
SAM PHILLIPS RECORDING SERVICE

As he picked cotton alongside his sharecropper parents in Florence, Alabama, a young Sam Phillips listened intently to the songs the black laborers sang in the fields. He learned a particular "natural" form of rhythm from them that influenced every step of his professional life. At age sixteen, a visit to Beale Street made a similar deep impression. Before too long, Phillips was on the radio sending music across the airwaves by both white and black musicians.

Phillips opened The Memphis Recording Service (MRS), the city's first recording studio, just before his twenty-seventh birthday in 1950. "January first in 1950 was the beginning of his lease. That really hits me because that's the very first day of the second half of the twentieth century. It's like Before Sam Phillips and After Sam Phillips in American music," says local musician Memphis Jones, who performs many of the legendary songs that Phillips recorded weekly on Beale Street. In the early days, the modest studio recorded speeches and even weddings. Phillips worked with local rhythm and blues artists as well, and leased the tracks to record labels. In 1952, he launched his own label, Sun Studio. The Memphis Recording Service continued as his label's recording studio, and captured the timeless voices of Elvis Presley, Johnny Cash, Jerry Lee Lewis, Carl Perkins, B.B. King, and Howlin' Wolf.

Phillips valued simplicity. To differentiate himself from Nashville's studios, he focused on a "blues feel" in the music. He searched for original compilations that demonstrated the shared spirit between white and black people, because he believed more similarities existed than differences. Much to the chagrin of white society, Phillips recorded many black artists, and was always keenly aware of the need to overcome society's racial barriers. "He was recording people that nobody else would record. He did it intentionally because he said right here in Memphis was an entire race of people that were not given a chance to prove themselves," Jones says admiringly. "He had this idea of people telling their own story. As that developed, that's where he got the idea of a white kid singing the blues. He grew up poor, so he knew that... the general rule was that poor whites and poor blacks lived together."

Phillips discovered Elvis in 1954. After months of work and frustrations, Phillips, Elvis, and his team finally created something distinctly different: music with a black "feel," but with a blended variety of so much else that made it truly unique. Elvis embodied the unity between the races Phillips wanted. "He [Phillips] proved that the music he was looking for, that unity he was trying to define, was what the world wanted," says Jones.

Phillips was known for not just a Southern preacher's cadence, but also for his ability to reach down into the soul of an artist and draw out their truest music. Memphis drummer and sound engineer, Richard Rosebrough, who worked at Sam Phillips Recording Studio from 1977 to 1984, witnessed Phillips' qualities in action. "He [Phillips] was invited down to a session for John Prine for the "Pink Cadillac" album in 1977. The band selected a number titled "Saigon" but Mr. Phillips thought they played it too fast and he made them slow it down and play it slower and slower until it was painful," Rosebrough says and recalls that some of them thought Phillips was joking; but, he was very serious. "He also kept pushing down the talk-back button which cut off all of their microphones and made them mad." This was how the Sam Phillips magic happened. Rosebrough continues, "When Sam knew the time was right, he backed off and told them they could play it a little faster. The result was miraculously inspired and full of energy and it had what it needed to be a viable record. Sam knew what he wanted and he got it. Very memorable."

Phillips went on to discover and draw out great musical talents at Sun Studio. By 1957, the association between Sun and rock and roll was so strong that Phillips developed a more diverse label dubbed Phillips International. In 1958, he felt the need for larger recording space, offices, and room for multi-track recorders. He chose the building at 639 Madison Avenue, which formerly housed a Midas Muffler Shop and a bakery, for his new endeavor. The former Sun Studio building became a scuba shop and a car garage.

The interior of the new establishment had to be gutted and rebuilt before he could open the doors of Sam Phillips Recording Service. Phillips paid particular attention to the design as well as the technology. The "space age" look was reminiscent of a 1950s Buick, with its curved lines and unique touches like Phillips' jukebox office desk. For Rosebrough the studio's interior is itself inspirational. "Phillips Recording is

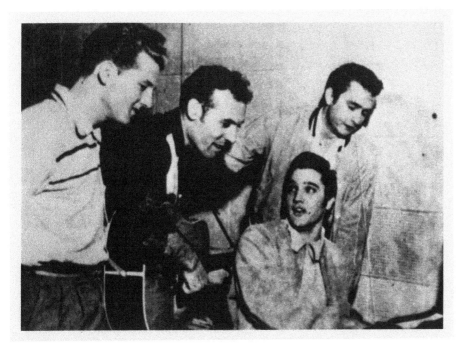

Sun Studio Session with Jerry Lee Lewis, Carl Perkins, Elvis Presley and Johnny Cash. **Memphis and Shelby County Room, Memphis Public Library & Information Center.**

Scotty Moore and James V. Roy at the 25th anniversary event at Sun Studios. **Courtesy of James V. Roy.**

wonderfully and beautifully designed in classic '50s décor, complete with curving walls, angular rooms and nautilus lighting in the penthouse suite... It has been said that walking through Phillips Studio is like standing on a Hollywood Street corner during its heyday. It is a very imaginative place, perfect for an artist," he says.

The state-of-the-art studio opened in 1960. Roughly a decade later, Phillips exited the music industry, and left "Memphis Sound" to other studios like Goldwax Records, Hi, and, of course, Stax. Phillips' son, Knox, continues his father's legacy as the owner of Sam Phillips Recording Service. Retooled in 1995, the studio kept the analog equipment. Today's artists can achieve a unique sound with the analog recording and the studio's design. Rosebrough

explains how sound can be altered by adjusting some of the moving parts in the room, "Two of the walls have floor to ceiling door panels that, when opened, reduce the reverberation and give the room a deader sound. When the doors are closed, a hard reflective surface results in a more live sounding room. By opening the panel doors on the 'back wall' of the room, a cavity is created that changes the volume and acoustic characteristic of the room." As a result, the "sound in studio A at Phillips is very characteristic and recognizable."

The MRS "record anything, anytime, anywhere" philosophy lives on at Sam Phillips. Carolyn Jensen recalls how meaningful it was for her 82-year-old mother to record her own album. In 2007, Mary Vaughn Webb recorded a few of her favorite songs from the forties and fifties, as well as one she herself wrote, at Sam Phillips Recording. When they walked in, Jensen and her mother saw Jerry Lee Lewis' piano and long-time Phillips' guitarist and engineer, Roland Janes, behind the sound board. Having sung with them around town before, Webb knew many of the famed musicians who played on her CD. "'My Buddy,' she did that one because of her best friend who died when she was in her forties... she thought of her," Jensen recalls. "She wanted to do her song that she wrote, and it's called 'Dreams Do Come True.' And that's the name of the CD." She continues, "Roland Janes cared, and he would say, 'okay let's do that again,' or 'I think we need to do this.'" Jensen's mother passed away a few years later. Recording at Sam Phillips was "the thrill of her life."

In 1979, Sun Studio reopened, a near

Sun artist party including music icons Scotty Moore, Isaac Hayes, Marshall Grant, Sam the Sham, and others. **James V. Roy.**

duplicate of what it was when Phillips and his musicians changed the world. The working studio and associated museum are among the most popular attractions for tourists and locals alike in Memphis. James Roy, curator of the legendary guitarist Scotty Moore's website, recalls the celebratory spirit that surrounded the fiftieth anniversary of Elvis' recording, "That's All Right, Mama." "It started with a Sun artist party the evening before and many of the major artists that recorded there or in the city attended. The following day I was one of the few non-officials inside the studio during the simultaneous broadcast of the song to many radios stations across the country commemorating the moment. That was followed by a day-long concert in front of the studio where Scotty was performing," Roy remembers. Although he spent considerable time at

Sun Studio before, the event was the most memorable he ever attended.

Phillips won numerous awards for his accomplishments, and became one of the first inductees in the Rock and Roll Hall of Fame in 1986. The awards do not do justice to his impact on the world. Phillips summed it up best in an interview given near the end of his life, "It changed the world, what we did at that little studio. I'm taking nothing away from all of the other great independent labels, but what we did managed to cut through the segregation to such an extent that it was way beyond what I had even hoped we could do. That not only affected this nation, it affected people around the world, and it absolutely had a lot to do with encouraging communication between people of different races."

Painting of B.B. King's Company Store sign on Beale Street. **Rebecca Phillips.**

"HE [KING] BASICALLY WANTS US TO BE AS

AUTHENTIC AS WE CAN AND PRESERVE THE BLUES."

— THOMAS PETERS

BEHIND THE NEON LIGHTS OF BEALE STREET AT B.B. KING'S

Beale Street gave him his big break and a world-renowned name. Decades later he would lend that name back to a struggling city, in an effort to preserve the history of the blues. The King of the Blues was born Riley B. King in 1925, on an Itta Bena, Mississippi, plantation in the heart of the Delta. As a young man, he played for tips on the street corner and had gigs in juke joints, sometimes playing in as many as four towns a night. Finally in 1947, at age 22, he hitchhiked his way to Memphis. His cousin, Bukka White, was the well-known blues musician who taught King the blues.

He eventually landed a regular show called "King's Spot" on WDIA, the first radio station with programming by African Americans for a black audience. His popularity demanded a DJ-worthy nickname. He was known for a time as, "Beale Street Blues Boy," which developed into, "Blues Boy King," and finally settled into, "B.B. King" – a name that stuck for the rest of his life. King started recording in 1949 and had a hit single, "Three O' Clock Blues," that landed at number one on the 1951 R&B charts. With another hit the following year, King launched into a demanding tour schedule that did not slow until recent years. He was inducted into the Blues Foundation Hall of Fame in 1984, and the Rock and Roll Hall of Fame in 1987. His influence over thousands of musicians is arguably greater than any other artist's.

Beale Street dates back to 1841, long before B.B. ever set foot there. It began as a mostly white commercial street with a row of antebellum mansions on the eastern end. The blues came in from the Delta at the turn of the century, causing Beale Street to gravitate towards entertainment. "[Blues] put down roots on Beale Street," says Memphis Jones, a regular musician at B.B. King's club. Beale was dubbed Negro Main Street of America in the 1920s, and it was said to eclipse New York City's Harlem. In 1924, a grocery store which doubled as a tobacco shop with fine cigars inhabited the buildings that now house B.B. King's club and store. A liquor store settled there in 1935. At some point the original building was torn down and rebuilt. Numerous African American doctors, lawyers, dentists, real estate agents, and other professionals, kept office space on the second floor of the new building. Beginning around the mid-1940s, people referred to it as the Colored Business Exchange Building.

Beale Street floundered until the city of Memphis asked Thomas Peters to open the flagship B.B. King's Blues Club in 1991. "At that point in time nobody was going to Beale Street," Peters recalls, "Everybody thought I was crazy." Beale endured fifteen years of club failures that could not accomplish what this blues club did – turn Beale Street into the state's top tourist destination. The club's success jumpstarted a Beale Street revival. In 2008, the "speakeasy" restaurant, Itta Bena, opened above the club, and serves classic Southern dishes to tourists and locals alike. Next door to the club, the B.B. King Company Store offers blues fans all manner of merchandise related to the King of the Blues.

The storefront of B.B. King's Company Store says, "Established in 1945," which refers to the year B.B. came to Beale. Sarah Wright, who has worked behind the gift shop counter for the past two and a half years, hears the stories of countless blues fans. Because of B.B.'s popularity in Europe, she often gets foreign currency from tourists, which she always enjoys. She meets famous musicians and athletes who make the pilgrimage to the club, but the regular Joes inspire her most. "My favorite stories are from people who've never been to Memphis before. They barely have the means to get here but somehow they make it. That's always the people I'm always drawn to because they have fun stories," she says, remembering one customer in particular whose story stuck with her. "I've met a terminally ill man named Bob from Minnesota who was eighty-something years old, never been to Memphis, and was just so tickled that he got the chance to come." She gave him a little memento so he could remember his trip and further recalls, "I cried my eyes out in the gift shop later on that night."

Thomas Peters carried out King's mission in every way possible, from the club's atmosphere to the scheduled acts. "He [King] basically wants us to be as authentic as we can and preserve the blues," Peters says. For Sarah Wright, there could be no better way than to do that than under the name of B.B. King. "Even though there are plenty of other blues musicians from Mississippi and the Delta area, he represents the blues for everybody... On top of that, I always have fans who come in and say 'I saw him two years ago, ten years ago, or fifty years ago.' And they'll say when they met him

afterwards that he's such a humble man. I've heard so many stories about how humble he is and I think that's why people want to support him and come here."

As she greets customers and hears their stories, Wright hears the club's music float through the narrow doorway. Twice a week the multi-talented Memphis Jones shares the history of blues and Memphis music with audiences at B.B. King's. "We're telling the history behind this amazing song they've been singing all their life and then we play it, and play it with excellence," Jones says, describing the show he and his bandmates stage.

Jones loves the history of both the music he plays and the history of the street where he plays it. "When B.B. King went down to Beale Street as a young man, they laughed him off the street. He said everybody on the street could play better than he did. So for him to be the one to get his name in lights on that street... that's bigger than a bar, bigger than a performance hall, bigger than a restaurant. There's a human aspect there that I really love about that place," Jones says, "It is his legacy." Every night the bright red light of B.B. King's name shines down on music lovers around the world who visit Beale Street. "The only Delta bluesman that ever had his name in neon on Beale Street," Jones concludes.

The blues forever altered the Beale Street vibe. To illustrate that fact, Jones quotes singer and entertainer, Rufus Thomas, "If you were black for one Saturday night and on Beale Street, never would you want to be white again." Jones explains the impact Beale had on Thomas, "He said when he was a kid, he could only go to the zoo one day of the week, on colored days. He could only do this, he could only do that... The world was closed to him as a young black man. But he said every Saturday night on Beale Street he could be exactly who he wanted to be and he was surrounded by a couple thousand other people who were having the exact same experience. He said it was the only place he could really be free. That's way deeper than barbecue or blues, that's a person's life. So I've got a lot of respect for Beale Street."

Jones also talks about the atmosphere when tired tourists head back to their hotel rooms and the locals own the street. "Memphis still comes out and South Memphis still comes out. The rap music is turned up and people are doing just weird stuff," he says with affection. "It still is Beale Street." For B.B. King, Beale Street always represented Memphis. In fact, he once said, "I didn't think of Memphis as Memphis. I thought of Beale Street as Memphis." As long as people like King, Peters, and Jones continue to respect and preserve the history and rhythm of the blues, this sentiment is likely to be shared by visitors and locals alike.

Beale and Second Street, 1970. The building on the corner of these streets became B.B. King's Blues Club and B.B. King's Company Store. **Memphis and Shelby County Room, Memphis Public Library & Information Center.**

"I DON'T THINK THEY KNEW THAT THEIR CREATION WOULD INSPIRE SO MANY LIVES. I AM PROUD TO BE A PART OF THAT HISTORY NOW." — LENORA GREEN

Soulsville U.S.A. sign on the Soulsville Charter School. The school is operated by the Soulsville Foundation which seeks to preserve and enrich the Soulsville history and community. **Rebecca Phillips.**

REDISCOVERING THE SOUL IN SOULSVILLE, U.S.A.

Jim Stewart and his sister, Estelle Axton, moved into the neighborhood now known as Soulsville, U.S.A., when other white people moved out of it. In 1959, they chose the abandoned Capitol Theater, located at 926 East McLemore Avenue, for their small recording business, Satellite Records. They originally focused on country western music but the influence of the black musicians who dropped into the studio shifted the sound toward rhythm and blues. In 1960, Memphis DJ Rufus Thomas, and his daughter, Carla Thomas, recorded the studio's first hit, "Cause I Love You." In 1961, Stewart and Axton combined their last names to create their new company label, Stax Records.

From 1961 to 1975, Stax cut eight hundred singles and three hundred albums. Their star-studded roster included Otis Redding, Sam and Dave, Eddie Floyd, the Bar-Kays, Booker T. and the MGs, Isaac Hayes, the Staple Singers, and so many others. While other black-oriented music such as Motown was known for a more polished style, Stax soul music had a strong beat and a certain kind of raw earthiness which soon became known as "Memphis Sound."

Executives and musicians at Stax focused on making amazing music in the studio. Their legacy became so much more than producing a whole lot of soul. At a time when segregation and inequalities tore the country apart, Stax was an example of what society could look like. "When we were working in this facility, race was never an issue," songwriter David Porter recalled in a 2004 Chicago Sun Times article. "Everybody bonded as a force factor for each other. True, when you're working fifteen hours a day, you don't get out in the streets to interact with what's going on. But we were tremendously loyal to each other inside the studio." He described what Stax was like, "We had a mostly black environment, but you had [whites] Steve Cropper, Duck Dunn, Wayne Jackson, a couple other horn players who were working every day in the studio. It was a very special bond." On April 4, 1968, the outside world caught up with the studio's magic and unity.

Stax's atmosphere changed after Dr. Martin

The Bar-Kays underneath the original Stax marquee, 1969. **Special Collections, University of Memphis Libraries.**

Luther King, Jr., was assassinated at the Lorraine Motel. The Lorraine provided a safe haven for black Stax musicians who stayed in Memphis; and it was one of the few places where whites and blacks could work together without trouble. As a result, many Stax hits were written at the upscale motel. For example, Eddie Floyd and Steve Cropper wrote "Knock on Wood" together at the Lorraine during a thunderstorm. "We had the melody down, but we struggled with the lyrics," Floyd recalled, "Steve and I had set out to write a song about superstition. But then there was a flash and a boom. That's when I came up with, 'It's like

thunder, lightning, the way you love me is frightening.'" Tensions mounted in the city of Memphis following Dr. King's assassination, and cast a shadow over everything, including harmonious places like Stax and the Lorraine.

The crisis in the civil rights movement left its mark on Stax. Al Bell, co-owner of Stax Records, described black artists who saw themselves as "picking up the baton" after Dr. King's assassination. The music began to reflect a new perspective on the world. The neighborhood near Stax became hostile toward the integrated business. David Porter described the change, "When Dr. King was shot, the

Exterior of Stax Records in 1976. **Special Collections, University of Memphis Libraries.**

community around us went in an uproar. People got bitter. It became stressful to come to work. Because of the uncomfortableness around us, that energy moved inside the building." The tension never caused a breakdown in the bonds between the artists but it did affect the work environment. "It did not damage the respect and loyalty for each other, it just damaged the climate in which we worked."

Financial troubles forced Stax into bankruptcy in 1975. The building went to the Southside Church of God and Christ, who planned to turn it into a community center. However, by 1989 the abandoned building fell into disrepair. Even though the community did not want to see it happen, Stax was razed to the ground. Very few original pieces remained from the demolition when the idea to rebuild it ten years later first came to fruition. Local historian Jimmy Ogle played a role in saving some of these original artifacts. "We cut out that tile façade, studs and all, and took it to the Mississippi River Museum for thirteen years. Nobody would've thought back then that Stax would've been rebuilt," Ogle explains, "We actually did the architectural drawings back then and saved them. That's how they rebuilt that in the same fashion." The red and white tile that spells "Stax Records Co.," is

Red and white tile artwork is the only piece from the original Stax Records building on the rebuilt version. **Jeremy Greene.**

the only piece of the original building on the rebuilt version. The original Stax signs are now in Alfred's and Rum Boogie on Beale Street.

In the late 1990s, a group of business leaders, philanthropists, and former Stax employees came together to form the Ewarton Foundation. The nonprofit entity continued a Stax tradition when it identified itself with yet another combination of Stax founders' last names. In 2005, it became the Soulsville Foundation, inspired by Stax Records' original Soulsville, U.S.A. marquee. Former Stax employee and then executive director of the foundation, Deanie Parker, explained the choice, "Everybody can relate to 'Soulsville.' People can relate to it as a place. It's something physical. It can be an attitude, and it certainly is music-related." The new logo for the foundation and the planned museum was a throwback to the original Stax Records' logo. "The finger snap says so much about soul and R&B. It's a symbol of how you feel when you hear the music. And it's so recognized around the world that it needed to be included in the museum logo," said Kimberly Brisco, the designer behind the new logo.

The Soulsville Foundation's mission is "to preserve, promote, and celebrate the many unique cultural assets of the Soulsville, U.S.A. neighborhood in Memphis, while supporting the development of new educational and community-building opportunities." With 14 million dollars in grants and six million dollars in seed money from anonymous donors, the foundation purchased the lot where Stax once stood, as well as some of the surrounding land. The City of Memphis, Shelby County, and the Federal Government provided additional

funding, with grants of three million dollars each. Other backing came from foundations, corporations, and individuals. The foundation oversees the major elements that now make up the heart of Soulsville: The Stax Music Academy, Stax Museum of American Soul Music, and The Soulsville Charter School.

In June of 2000, a group of at-risk children gathered in the Stafford Elementary cafeteria for the inaugural Stax Music Academy. In 2002, the academy acquired its own building on the Soulsville complex, filled with dedicated practice rooms, choir and band suites, and an array of classrooms. Students from the charter school next door, already bursting at the seams with success, used some of the space. Adrianna Christmas, Program Manager and Vocal Instructor, feels at home working with the students in the academy. "About 65 percent of our students qualify for free or reduced lunch, many come from single-parent homes like I did, and have all kinds of things going on in their personal lives," she says, explaining the typical students' background. "However, no matter what they are dealing with, they just light up when they come here because they know it is a place of release and self-expression," Christmas says. Fourteen years after its early stages in borrowed space, the program has grown to serve a record-breaking 120 after-school students and 95 summer program students.

Students must audition for the program. Once accepted they learn everything from music theory and marketing to music law. They can record their own music and have access to a media room for post-production work. Lenora Green is a student at LeMoyne-Owen College and the current artist-in-residence at the academy. She came to Memphis unsure of what her long-neglected, new community would be like. She quickly realized she connected with students at the highest levels. "I came from a school where I had to deal with drugs, gang violence and lack of information about where the next step should be in my life. But I found music to be my niche," Green explains, "For a singer, 'perfect placement' happens when the sound of your voice resonates in the right place in your body for it to be carried in a bigger space to fill up a room. Soulsville is like that for me. I'm able to help students find the 'soul' of their voice through academia, business tactics and professionalism especially when a student expresses that he or she has an interest in studying music."

Following the start of Stax Music Academy in 2001, the foundation hosted a "Ground Shakin' Ground Breakin'" ceremony where the Stax Museum of American Soul Music now stands. When the museum opened in 2003, Memphis celebrated with performances and events all around town. A museum now stands where there was once a lonely historical marker on an empty lot, and honors those who sacrificed to create music that united the country. "Even though they've redone it [Stax Records], they've kept it funky. That's the best word to describe it," says Maggie Russell of the Soulsville Foundation. Speakers pump soul music across the parking lot, surrounding students and visitors with the voices of legends. In admiration of the museum, Russell says, "they could portray it so many different ways, but they do such a great job of preserving it. It's not depressing but it doesn't make it into something it's not."

Clearly, memorabilia isn't the most important part of the foundation's preservation efforts. Rather, it's ensuring the soul of Stax lives on in the community's students. Inside the museum, the replica of Studio A is one place to see this at work. On Tuesday afternoons during June and July, the Stax Music Academy Alumni Band fills the packed room with soul music again. Russell clearly loves these performances. "They sound just like it. It's one thing to sing the song and another to actually *feel* it and sing it. And they feel it!"

In 2005, The Soulsville Charter School (TSCS) started with a class of 60 sixth graders. Each year added another class until the tuition-free school served sixth through twelfth grades. In 2011, students moved into their own fifty-thousand-square-foot building on Soulsville grounds. The curriculum is challenging even without the added obstacle of students starting as much as two years behind. In 2012, the first graduating class attained one hundred percent college acceptance and won millions in scholarships. The "Soulsville 51" met many film crews and Stax greats, like James Alexander and Larry Dodson of the Bar-Kays, who held an impromptu jam session with students. One hundred percent of the 2013 and 2014 classes were also accepted to college. In total, the three graduating classes have, to this date, earned 20 million dollars in scholarships and grants.

Walking the halls of TSCS, it is clear more goes on there than just academics and music. The students form teams and compete for the highest grades or best attendance. The winning teams' pictures are proudly displayed on the

Stax Music Academy sign above the reception desk. **Jeremy Greene.**

wall. Attendance percentages, high test scores, and poster projects that detail students' summer growth experiences line the halls. Sunlight struggles to pierce through the downstairs window, completely covered with seniors' college acceptance letters. Russell describes the charter school's version of a college signing day. "They get a poster and they decorate it with the school that they were accepted to, they pick a walk out song." Over deafening cheers, the emcee names all the colleges that accepted each student, in addition to his or her scholarship amounts. When asked which school the graduate chose, each senior pops open the poster and proclaims his or her new school. The crowd erupts in cheers for each and every student.

Nothing illustrates the spirit of support, encouragement, and community that bursts from every inch of the school quite like the tradition of "snapping." Russell experienced the phenomenon when she toured the school on one of her first days with the foundation. She walked into a math competition in a classroom where two students, one from each of two "teams," worked out a problem on the board. They raced each other to solve the problem and move their team ahead. "They're both at the board... and she starts counting on her fingers, she's having trouble, and she's erasing it... she's struggling. And so some of the kids start snapping," Russell explains. While the uninitiated might think the snapping signals impatience, at Soulsville it is a sign of celebration and encouragement. The snap is deeply rooted in the history of Soulsville, U.S.A. In fact, it is the Stax Records logo. "She didn't win, but every single kid on both sides was clapping. The kid standing next to her stood there and waited for her to finish, and kind of coached her a little bit on what to do," Russell says smiling at the memory. "It wasn't about who won what. It was that you helped each other. And eventually she got it." Everybody from teachers and administrators to students, snap to recognize anything positive.

All this happened on a little corner in Memphis, on a lot that Tim Sampson, Communications Director for the Soulsville Foundation, once described as an "urban war zone." Sampson remembered, "The original Stax Records building had been demolished a decade earlier and the site was nothing but a weeded, cracked-concrete empty lot covered with broken glass and garbage. Next door to the lot, where the Stax Music Academy now stands, was an abandoned 65-unit apartment building with no windows and knee-high trash in every unit," he said, acknowledging that the success stories are only possible because of the original Stax artists who came before them. "We know we stand

on their shoulders," he wrote for the *Memphis Flyer* days after the charter school celebrated its first graduation. Lenora Green echoes those sentiments, "I don't think they knew that their creation would inspire so many lives. I am proud to be a part of that history now."

Just around the corner from Stax Records stands The Four Way, yet another testament to the strong community roots of Soulsville, U.S.A. Now owned by Willie Earl Bates, the restaurant's soul food and rich history are an important part of Soulsville. Bates grew up near the restaurant and has a deep appreciation for his community. When Clint and Irene Cleaves first purchased the place in 1946, the restaurant was little more than a few tables in a pool hall. They soon expanded into a full service establishment that served casual fare at the front counter with fine dining in a back room accessible only by ringing a doorbell. Because Cleaves was also E.H. "Boss" Crump's chauffeur, Crump sent his friends to eat at The Four Way. The restaurant was unlike anywhere else in Memphis. Blacks and whites ate there together any day of the week. "This restaurant has been integrated from day one," Bates explains. In 1996, The Four Way closed because Mrs. Cleaves' failing health kept her away from the business. Attempts were made to save the restaurant but it did not get back its true soul until Bates learned he had the opportunity to buy it.

"I searched my heart and my thoughts in terms of its past history and the sacrifice of Dr. King who ate here on a regular basis, the community where persons gathered, in this area, for social joys and reunion," Bates says, regarding his decision to reopen The Four Way. In 2002, he welcomed eager customers back into the restaurant and began a partnership with other community stalwarts. "We do have the support of the community, and even in the midst of redevelopment where we are, too, a part of Soulsville, but yet to blossom. And so to be able to have that type of experience and be able to have that type of support is strictly special," Bates says.

Today the community witnesses the rebirth of Soulsville, U.S.A., a place where a white brother and sister fell in love with R&B, a group of musicians inadvertently changed the world, and education rebuilds a broken community. This place always was, and always will be, a team effort. Carrying out the dream of Dr. King is, "no one person's journey. It's everybody who will, and everybody who can, to add to, wherever they are. It's a price you pay for living, and I enjoy it," Bates says, "Actually, individuals did so much for me in the community when I came along. So, it's a matter of giving back." This driving force motivates him to get up early and work late. He adds, "To be able to keep going is a signal... that we're on the right track... that we're making a difference."

Painting of the Chicago Pizza Factory sign. After closing, the restaurant remain

ant for many years with all seats, tables and décor left behind. **Rebecca Phillips.**

OVERTON SQUARE, WHERE MIDTOWN IS MEMPHIS

Before partiers spent the seventies discoing at Sweet Caroline's, before anyone ever sat down to eat Chicago-style pizza, before a particular building stood empty for years, and long before diners could eat a taco and a hotdog in the same meal, the area known today as Overton Square was a cow field. When Elisabeth Griffin moved to the cottage with the white picket fence at 2118 Madison Avenue in 1919, only farms and Oliver's Confectionary operated nearby. Mr. Griffin joined her when they married in 1928. The Griffins saw every sort of possible transformation from their windows.

The early thirties saw the construction of buildings that made up the core of the square. Businesses included a paint store, a drugstore, and other mom-and-pop type places. When one of the earliest business owners in the area, Jimmy Mounce, wanted to open the Lobster Shack with Pappy Sammons, and asked for the Griffins' support, Elisabeth refused to sign his petition, citing "principles." Throughout the years, the Griffins fielded multiple offers for their property but they stayed, regardless of how noisy or busy the Square became. Their home stuck out amid the bars and restaurants and became so well-known that the post office once delivered a letter addressed simply to "the house across from Friday's with the picket fence." Considering their position on the subject, the Griffins became friends, oddly enough, with business owners like Mounce, and they considered Overton Square to be a positive aspect of the neighborhood. Stoy Bailey remembered Mrs. Griffin as a friendly, polite lady, "I would see her out in the yard... and you'd always stop and speak to Mrs. Griffin."

Overton Square got its name from the group of investors who created it. In the late 1960s, a rich, young friend-of-hippies, James D. "Jimmy" Robinson, Jr., opened a coffeehouse called Perception on Madison Avenue. His ideas for the area quickly surpassed the small hangout as soon as he experienced T.G.I. Fridays in New York City. Robinson and a group of investors (eventually incorporated as Overton Square, Inc.) acquired properties along Madison. In November, 1969, the city legalized the sale of liquor by the glass. The next day the group announced the Perception building would be a new combination bar and restaurant – T.G.I. Fridays.

A new era began on Overton Square when Fridays opened in May of 1970. Fridays was popular from day one. Robinson hoped to break even with eight hundred dollars a day. The first day (and every day until their expansion) the restaurant pulled in 4,800 dollars. Fridays was just the beginning. A 1969 news article that covered the Fridays announcement stated they would create a "multi-million-dollar development for the young-at-heart." Patrons often stood as much as five deep at the bar trying to catch the eye of one of the heartthrob bartenders. One can only imagine the chaos as bartenders handed out drinks and rang the bell to celebrate a tip having been received. To enhance the party-like atmosphere, the famously handsome bartenders danced and performed bottle tricks as they mixed drinks behind the bar.

Overton Square grew as more restaurants, bars, music venues, and retail locations opened. With the opening of Lafayette's Music Room, Overton Square became a true music and entertainment district. One night Billy Joel, who often played in Memphis, staged a free concert that lasted until three in the morning. The event ended when the fire department appeared; there were so many people trying to get into the show it became a hazard.

The seventies were Overton Square's heyday. "The good times are rolling at Memphis' version of Greenwich Village, Bourbon Street, and Gatlinburg all rolled into one." A *Memphis Press-Scimitar* article described. "You would go there every night and see the same people... it sort of became a little community," Dianne Pendergrass said of the square's atmosphere. Stoy Bailey echoes the sentiment. "It was the sort of place where you didn't necessarily have to go into a club or into a store or anything. There were places you could just sit. I met a lot of people," Bailey recalls of his "wandering" days on Overton Square.

Retailers like John Simmons introduced new experiences like art shows to the city's younger demographic. Realtor Jeanne Arthur recalled Simmons hosting one of the first art shows in Memphis, "He was the first to have shows for Mary Sims and Sophie Coors. And everybody would go crazy going to those, because back then young people had never really thought about buying art." "Whatever he touched turned to gold," recalls June West of Simmons' retail prowess. Riding the wave of popularity with the younger set, Sweet Caroline's opened in 1972. The disco bar that would later become Chicago Pizza Factory was named after owner, Taylor Caruthers' mother.

Just five years after its grand opening in 1975, Overton Square developers announced expansion plans. As developer Benjamin Woodson described, "The plan ultimately is to have a complete micro-community where

T.G.I. Fridays in 1977. The popular restaurant opened soon after liquor by the glass became legal in the state of Tennessee. **Memphis and Shelby County Room, Memphis Public Library & Information Center.**

people can work, live, shop, and play – all in an environment that provides unique and superior esthetics in a... desirable location." The proposal called for more specialty retail, an addition to T.G.I. Fridays, an "open mall" area, office buildings, and a hotel, among other features.

In 1976, revelers eagerly awaited the inaugural snowfall of the "Charles Dickens Christmas" at Overton Square. Carolers sang along the street in nineteenth century costumes. An outdoor skating rink between Cooper and Florence streets attracted all ages. Horse-drawn carriages, a merry-go-round, and sleigh and pony rides were available to heighten the Christmas spirit. The stage was set. All they needed was low enough temperatures, specifically 28 degrees

or below, for the snow-maker attached to the fire hydrants, to work. As soon as temperatures reached that magic number, two inches of ice and snow covered Overton Square. The following year an indoor skating rink opened. Overton Square was so popular the city of Memphis held the annual Christmas parade on Madison Avenue. The official city Christmas tree stood in front of Fridays.

In 1977, skaters formed tight circles and skated around the small rink inside Overton Square Gardens while shops overlooked the ice from the second floor. "It was so crowded you could barely move, and the ice quickly became grooved so when you fell, your knees took a terrible battering from those ice ridges," Bonnie

The indoor ice skating rink is one of the most memorable features of Overton Square's past. **Special Collections, University of Memphis Libraries.**

Kourvelas recounted. A new courtyard, which featured a bell tower as its crowning jewel, was in the works behind the skating rink. In 1982 the skating rink became the Rialto-Palm Court, a restaurant and culinary supermarket, which cost roughly $300,000.

The late seventies saw the beginnings of a passing era. In 1976, community staple Burkle's Bakery, open since before Overton Square's creation, closed its doors. Over a thousand customers made their final visit on Burkle's last day. In 1979, Overton Square business owners fêted Lehman C. Sammons, proprietor of Pappy's Lobster Shack, on his hundredth birthday. Pappy was proclaimed "Mayor of Overton Square," a title he held for a few months before he passed away. His daughter attempted to keep the restaurant open but it was shuttered in 1980.

In 1979, Caroline's Disco became Chicago Pizza Factory. The new restaurant was run by Caruthers' father, Jerry. The pizza parlor quickly became a "local landmark... not so much for its Italianesque fare but for its vibrant atmosphere and movie-marquee-style flashing light signage." The iron arch with bright yellow letters spelled out "Chicago" and welcomed many a diner to his or her first taste of deep dish pizza. "It was kind of a novelty thing. It was exciting to get to go and try out what the Chicago pan pizza was all about. It was something totally different than any of us in that part of the country had ever experienced before," Dianne Pendergrass remembers about her first taste of deep dish, "With the pizza coming in a pan and it was just really thick and loaded... it was just a different eating experience." Chicago Pizza Factory's

pizza wasn't what made an impression on young Drew Whooten. Instead, he remembers the décor, "They had pictures of people that had eaten there and I think Boston College came to the Liberty Bowl and Doug Flutie's picture was up there. I thought that was so cool that he could've been sitting where I was."

Overton Square faced a "slow demise" in the eighties. The city's renewed focus on downtown development, namely Beale Street and the riverfront, created entertainment competition. Once the original investors sold the property, the team spirit and passion for the area's development waned. "Ben [Woodson] was able to make it more of a community," June West explains, "People from all the neighborhoods would walk there to participate. They had community events... they had an ice skating rink when no one was doing that. So it was really top-notch." New investors, however, could not achieve the same community atmosphere as their predecessors, and their attempts to generate enthusiasm among retailers and clientele failed.

In July of 1983, the music club, Solomon Alfred's, closed, which paved the way for a new expansion plan aimed at saving Overton Square – a "French Quarter-style hotel." Before it closed, Solomon's hosted one of the most memorable moments on the square for Pendergrass. In 1981, *General Hospital* aired one of the show's most popular and long-awaited episodes – the Luke and Laura wedding. Solomon's invited everyone to celebrate the marriage with them. She remembers, "It was this huge episode of *General Hospital*... and they threw this party. They had wedding cake... we all

Above: *Overton Square regular walking beside the neighborhood drunk.* **Stoy Baily.**

Below: *New tenants and artwork on Overton Square, 2014.* **Jeremy Greene.**

watched the wedding. It was kind of weird but a lot of fun!"

The Chicago Pizza Factory building echoed Overton Square's decline. Emptied of diners in 1989, it stood vacant for decades with only the unlit neon sign as a reminder of what it once was. "The Square was dying – they closed Fridays and Silky's, and everything went towards Beale Street. (My dad) locked the door and didn't go back in there for a long time," Caruthers said of that time. Even though 1992 was a record year for Overton Square, its image remained as a "struggling" area. Not until a renewed focus on the revitalization of the square would hungry Memphians walk underneath the Chicago Pizza Factory archway again.

In 2009, an investment company filed for a permit to demolish buildings at Madison and Cooper in order to erect five new structures, one of which would be a grocery store. The preservation organization, Memphis Heritage, raced to fight the proposal and keep the historic buildings. Executive Director June West led the charge for the community. "It wasn't just Memphis Heritage. We are the spark... Everything else is coordinated around people's interests, concerns, and passion," she explains. Just two years later, an entirely new focus and a new developer kickstarted the square's transformation into its current form.

Loeb Properties unveiled a new plan for Overton Square in 2011 which did not involve demolition, rather it contained an arts and entertainment theme and some new construction. "There are a lot of differences between Overton Square now and when it first redeveloped in the seventies. One is the theater

district is much stronger," West noted. This time around, the Studio on the Square movie theater, and the Playhouse on the Square live theater, serve as anchors for the district. One of the few black repertory theaters in the country, the Hattiloo, made Overton Square its home. Boutique retailers and restaurants round out these theaters. A large parking garage supports the crowds that come to enjoy the arts and outdoor entertainment, made possible by raised bandstands in the courtyard.

Overton Square was fairly empty throughout Taylor Berger's childhood. The darkness of the deserted, grotto-like patio and fascinating empty pizza parlor had a certain draw. "It [Chicago Pizza Factory] had this awesome looking patio that was all overgrown. You look inside and the tables were set up and everything looked ready to go, except for it was all spider webs... it was totally closed." One day Berger saw a For Lease sign on the abandoned building and immediately got to thinking. Given the "rumblings" of new things coming to Overton Square, Berger worked on his new restaurant concept, Chiwawa.

The extensive renovations that turned the building into Berger's Chiwawa included a signage change. Frank Balton Sign Company renovated the iconic iron archway at a cost of approximately 6,500 dollars. The archway returned to Overton Square with new, chasing lights and the phrase, "Midtown is Memphis" replaced "Chicago." Robin Balton, co-owner of Frank Balton Sign Company, observed "to spend that kind of money, it's very unusual, to not actually put your name up there and use it for advertising." The sign was meant to capture much more than just the Chiwawa brand.

Unbeknownst to Berger, John Branston, Tom Foster, and Calvin Turley coined the "Midtown is Memphis" phrase in 1993 in an effort to promote Midtown. Many t-shirts and bumper stickers have sported the line for decades. Branston described the phrase as short enough for a bumper sticker and long enough to encompass their Midtown pride, "Midtown is a slice of Memphis that represents history, proud tradition, black and white people, and old schools," he stated. When Berger learned the phrase's origin, he was happy to promote its creators. He framed the original *Memphis Magazine* article about the phrase's creators and displayed it in the restaurant. "When they found out we were going to use the phrase again on the sign they were very nice and supportive," says Berger.

It seems there may be no better place for such a sign than on Overton Square, at a restaurant that serves both tacos and hotdogs. With its storied (and sometimes checkered) past, beautiful historical buildings, and a lone yellow cottage with a white picket fence, the square has been full of hopes and dreams since it first came to life in the mind of Jimmy Robinson.

Midtown is Memphis arched sign, 2014. The Chicago Pizza Factory building and arched sign were remodeled by Chiwawa's owner. **Jeremy Greene.**

SUMMER AVE

SAM COOPER BLVD

N. McLEAN

TILLMAN

HIGHLAND

PANTAZE

R

PANTAZE DRUGS

WALNUT GROVE

N. COOPER

E. PKWY

COOPER ST.

MT. MORIAH

UNG AVE.

Shop SOUTHERN AVE.

Normal

1	UNIVERSAL LIFE INSURANCE CO.	**7**	DRINK-N-DRAG	**13** SKATELAND
2	ADVANCE RUBBER STAMPS	**8**	LAMAR THEATER	**14** LORRAINE MOTEL
3	ARCADE RESTAURANT	**9**	WALKER RADIATOR WORKS	**15** SAM PHILLIPS RECORDING SERVICE
4	THE BEAUTY SHOP	**10**	LOVE'S FEED	**16** B.B. KINGS
5	JOE'S WINES & LIQUORS	**11**	NORMAL BEAUTY SHOP	**17** SOULSVILLE, U.S.A.
6	CASEY'S MOTEL	**12**	LEAHY'S TRAILER PARK	**18** OVERTON SQUARE

Bibliography

CHAPTER ONE

"Back at Work Today – Universal Life Co. Ends 2-Day Dedication of New Building." *Memphis Press-Scimitar*, July 9, 1949.

Bates, Willie. Interview by Caitlin L. Horton and Rebecca Phillips. May 23, 2014.

Brooks, W. L., Jr., and J. T. Chandler. "Forty-five Interesting Years." *The ULICO*, Fall 1973.

David Flaum. "UL to Knock on Different Doors." *The Commercial Appeal*, September 8, 1985.

Find a Grave. "Dr Joseph Edison Walker, I." R. Wheaton. Accessed June 9, 2014. http://www.findagrave .com/cgi-bin/fg.cgi?page=gr&GRid=83107529.

Flynn, David. "Economic Roadblock is Next." *Memphis Press-Scimitar*, April 24, 1973.

Gause, Carolyn. "Black Insurance Firm Ranks 4th in Nation." *The Commercial Appeal*, October 14, 1979.

Gilliam, Art. Interview by Caitlin L. Horton. June 10, 2014.

Gilliam, Art. "The Significance of Maceo Walker." *The Commercial Appeal*, March 25, 1973.

"Historic Downtown." *The Daily News*, July 15, 1983.

"New Home Office of the Universal Life Insurance Co." *The ULICO*, Fall 1973.

Olive, B. G., Jr. "Looking Back on the Insurance Business." *The ULICO*, Fall 1973.

"Service to Area Spans Barriers." *The Commercial Appeal*, July 16, 1966.

Tucker, Jimmie. Interview by Caitlin L. Horton. December 20, 2013.

Tucker, Jimmie. "The Architect as Developer, If Walls Could Talk…" SlideShare. Accessed June 9, 2014. http://fr.slideshare.net/JTuckerAIA/universal-life-insurance-bldg.

"Universal Life Insurance Company." Historical marker Tennessee Historical Commission. *Universal Life Insurance Company*, 4E 131.

Williams, Nat D. "Dr. Walker – From Poverty, Obscurity to Success." *The ULICO*, Fall 1973.

CHAPTER TWO

"Glossary." *Customer Rubber Stamp Designer*. Accessed February 12, 2014. http://www .customrubberstampsdesigner.co.uk/glossary.html.

Hopalong Cassidy. "The Legend." Accessed February 6, 2014. http://www.hopalong.com/legend.htm.

Memphis Chamber of Commerce. "Shining Lights." *Memphis Greets You, Memphis Chamber of Commerce.* Dixon-Paul Printing Company, 1917.

Smith, Jeremy. E-mail to Rebecca Phillips. January 16, 2014.

Smith, Jeremy. Interview by Rebecca Phillips. March 24, 2014.

CHAPTER THREE

Bailey, Stoy. Interview by Caitlin L. Horton. May 15, 2014.

Friends for Our Riverfront. "Alley Naming & Walking Tour Honors Jack Tucker." Accessed June 9, 2014. http://www.friendsforourriverfront.org/2010/04/alley-naming-walking-tour-honors-jack_01.html.

Go South Main. "South Main: The Historic District." Accessed June 9, 2014. http://www.gosouthmain.com/history.html.

Historic-Memphis. "Historic Memphis... South Main Historic Arts District." Accessed June 9, 2014. http://historic-memphis.com/memphis-historic/arts/arts.html.

Historic-Memphis. "Memphis Main Street...in Vintage Postcards and Photos." Accessed June 9, 2014. http://historic-memphis.com/memphis-historic/mainstreet/mainstreet.html.

Jackson, Vicki. Interview by Rebecca Phillips. May 22, 2014.

Memphis Downtown Neighborhood Association. "Our History." Accessed June 9, 2014. http://www.memphisdna.org/about-us/history.

Ogle, Jimmy. Interview by Caitlin L. Horton and Rebecca Phillips. May 27, 2014.

Sells, Toby. "$outh Main." *Memphis Flyer*, May 22, 2014. Accessed June 9, 2014. http://www.memphisflyer.com/memphis/outh-main/Content?oid=3674230.

The City of Memphis. "History of Memphis." Accessed June 9, 2014. www.memphistn.gov/Visitors/MovingtoMemphis/HistoryofMemphis.aspx.

CHAPTER FOUR

"Arcade Brings Back Memories." *The Daily News*, May 6, 1988.

Baker, Sarah. "Got a Light?" *Memphis Flyer*, March 20-26, 1997.

Brown, Fred. "City Heritage Nourished at Arcade." *Memphis Memphis Press-Scimitar*, June 14, 1983.

Callahan, Jody. "Butcher Shop Manager Eyes Arcade." *The Commercial Appeal*, July 6, 1995.

Callahan, Jody. "Heartbreak Cafe: Arcade, Downtown Staple, Closing." *The Commercial Appeal*, December 14, 1996.

Collins, Chris. Email to Rebecca Phillips. May 7, 2014.

Ebert, Roger. "Mystery Train." RobertEbert.com. Accessed June 21, 2014. http://www.rogerebert.com/reviews/great-movie-mystery-train-1989.

Get Down Memphis. "Arcade Restaurant." Accessed June 9, 2013. www.downtownmemphis.com/directory/arcade-restaurant.

Miller, Kate. "Arcade Restaurant Bought Back by Zepatos at Large Discount." *Memphis Business Journal*, June 20, 2002. http://www.bizjournals.com/memphis/stories/2002/01/21/story3.html.

Miller, Kate. "Downtown's Arcade Restaurant to Change Ownership – Again." *Memphis Business Journal*, June 6, 2002. http://www.bizjournals.com/memphis/stories/2002/01/07/story3.html.

Putnam, Sue. "Mission Possible." Memphis Flyer, April 4-10, 1996.

Thomas, William. "Brick by Brick, Shrine Called Arcade Falls." *The Commercial Appeal*, March 16, 1993.

Zepatos, Harry, Jr. Interview by Rebecca Phillips. May 11, 2014.

CHAPTER FIVE

Andreini, Sharon. Interview by Caitlin L. Horton. March 27, 2014.

Carrier, Karen. Interview by Caitlin L. Horton. March 27, 2014.

Kemp, Kathy. *The Beauty Box: A Tribute to the Legendary Beauty Parlors of the South*. Birmingham: Crane Hill Publishers, 1997.

Tucker, Robin. Interview by Caitlin L. Horton. March 26, 2014.

CHAPTER SIX

Balton, Jeff. Interview by Rebecca Phillips. November 21, 2013.

"Joe's Wines and Liquors Going Retro and Cosmic with Renovations." *Memphis Business Journal*, November 9, 2009. http://www.bizjournals.com/memphis/stories/2009/11/16/tidbits1.html.

Jones, John. "Joe's Wines & Liquor." *John Jones Architect*. Accessed June 8, 2014. http://johnjonesarchitect.com/joes.

Larson, Brad Larson. Interview by Rebecca Phillips. November 8, 2013.

Milks, Warren. "Most Modern Concepts of Spectacular Lighting Application."

Seltzer, Debra Jane. Interview by Caitlin L. Horton. January 17, 2014.

Seltzer, Debra Jane. "Roto-Spheres." Roadside Architecture. Accessed June 8, 2014. http://www.agilitynut .com/sca/roto.html.

CHAPTER SEVEN

"Country Musician, Companion Slain." *The Dispatch*, November 20, 1973.

"Elvis Presley Boulevard." *The Commercial Appeal*, January 7, 1977.

Elvis Presley Boulevard Improvements. "Overview." Accessed February 19, 2014. http:// www.epbmemphis.com/overview.asp.

Flickr. "Casey's Motel Highway 51, Memphis, TN." Postcard. 1950s. *Birch from Memphis*. Accessed February 14, 2014. http://www.flickr.com/photos/51992558@N00/6214278006.

Flickr. "Rose Court." Postcard. Late 1930s. *Birch from Memphis*. Accessed February 14, 2014. http://www .flickr.com/photos/51992558@N00/6902039004.

"Improvements in Store for the Road to Graceland." *Associated Press*. Accessed February 19, 2014. http:// bigstory.ap.org/article/improvements-store-road-graceland.

"Motel Clerk No Fall Guy." *The Commercial Appeal*, August 1, 1971.

Nichols, Shawn. E-mail to Rebecca Phillips. December 14, 2013.

Perkins, Pamela. "Arrests, Closing of Motel Puts Focus on Prostitution Strip." *The Commercial Appeal*, December 5, 2002.

"Ripoff on the Boulevard." *The Commercial Appeal*, May 6, 1978.

"Sentence Given in Stars' Death." *Lawrence Journal-World*, November 6, 1974.

"South Bellevue Renamed Elvis Presley Boulevard." *The Commercial Appeal*, June 30, 1971.

"Tables Turned." *The Commercial Appeal*, April 7, 1976.

The Tune In. "Peter Cooper on Music: 1973 Killings Brought Fear to Nashville." Blog. Accessed November 10, 2013. http://blogs.tennessean.com/tunein/2013/11/10/peter-cooper-on-music-1973-killings-brought-fear-to-nashville.

CHAPTER EIGHT

Adelman, Erin Marie. E-mail to Rebecca Phillips. February 25, 2014.

Anonymous signmaker. Interview by Rebecca Phillips. May 16, 2014.

Club Spectrum Memphis. Website. Accessed June 9, 2014. http://www.thespectrummemphis.com.

Dries, Bill. "Downtown Dolls Loses Courtroom Battle." *The Daily News* 123, no. 147. July 29, 2008.

Erskine, Michael. "Exotic Dance Club is Still Open Despite Lawsuits." *The Commercial Appeal*, December 16, 2007.

Gilbert, Debbie. "The Rainmaker." Film Vault. Accessed June 9, 2014. http://www.filmvault.com/filmvault/memphis/r/rainmakerthe1.html.

Internet Movie Database. "The Rainmaker." Accessed June 9, 2014. http://www.imdb.com/title/tt0119978.

Keeter, Terry. "Baldwin Doubts Owens is on the Run." *The Commercial Appeal*, August 27, 1982.

McPeak, Alex. E-mail to Caitlin L. Horton. February 25, 2014.

Nazarian, Anahid. E-mail to Caitlin L. Horton. May 9, 2014.

Phillips, Rebecca. Interview by Caitlin L. Horton. May 9, 2014.

CHAPTER NINE

Badger, Clarence G. *The Campus Flirt*. Turner Classic Movies Website. Accessed June 7, 2014. http://www.tcm.com/tcmdb/title/492802/The-Campus-Flirt.

Bailey, Stoy. Interview by Caitlin L. Horton. May 15, 2014.

Beifuss, John. "Porn Star Harry Reems had Significant Ties to Memphis." *The Commercial Appeal*, March 20, 2013. http://www.commercialappeal.com/news/local-news/porn-star-harry-reems-had-significant-ties-to.

Bickers, Wilma. E-mail to Caitlin L. Horton. May 16, 2014.

Buckley, William, Jr. "'Deep Throat' Trial Issues Weighed." *Toledo Blade*, December 21, 1976.

Greaney, Devin. "Signs of the Times: What are the Stories Behind Memphis' Ghost Signs that Advertise to Another Era?" Devin Greaney website. Accessed June 7, 2014. http://www.devingreaney.samexhibit.com/pages/ghost-signs-of-memphis.

Klimek, Rose. E-mail to Caitlin L. Horton. May 17, 2014.

Knight, Connie. E-mail to Caitlin L. Horton. May 9, 2014.

Miller, Mary K. "It's a Wurlitzer." *Smithsonian Magazine*, June 7, 2014. http://www.smithsonianmag.com/history/its-a-wurlitzer-61398212/?no-ist.

Pruette, Barry. E-mail to Caitlin L. Horton. May 20, 2014.

CHAPTER TEN

"Custom Radiator Service Featured by Walker Shop." *The Commercial Appeal*, February 29, 1960.

Hot Rods and Custom Stuff. "1941 Clark Ford Truck." Accessed June 9, 2014. http://hotrodscustomstuff.com/projects/1941-clark-ford-truck.html.

Stone, Thomas. "A Hot Business in Custom-Made Radiators." *Memphis Business Journal*, March 26, 1984.

Walker, Harry. Interview by Caitlin L. Horton. May 29, 2014.

CHAPTER ELEVEN

Frey, Jennifer. Interview by Caitlin L. Horton. May 27, 2014.

Greene, Jeremy. E-mail to Caitlin L. Horton. June 5, 2014.

Love, Billy. Interview by Caitlin L. Horton. May 27, 2014.

Maple, Mike. "Mid-South Coliseum: Through the Years." *The Commercial Appeal*. Accessed June 8, 2014. http://www.commercialappeal.com/photos/galleries/2011/nov/27/mid-south-coliseum-through-years.

Ritter, Lindsay. "Truck Stop Moves Forward." Choose 901 website. Accessed June 8, 2014. http://www.choose901.com/truck-stop-approved-board-adjustment.

CHAPTER TWELVE

Bell, Shirley. Interview by Caitlin and Kennedy Horton. March 25, 2014.

Caldwell, Pauline. Interview by Caitlin and Kennedy Horton. March 25, 2014.

"College was Anchor of Normal Area." *The Commercial Appeal*, June 5, 2003.

Harder, Tom. E-mail to Caitlin L. Horton. June 9, 2014.

Hill, Margie. E-mail to Caitlin L. Horton. June 9, 2014.

Hoyle, Joseph. "This Group Will Talk About Old Days and the Dawn of Some Brighter Ones." *Memphis Press-Scimitar*, March 19, 1980.

Maxey, Ron. "Normal Station Lives Up to Name." *The Commercial Appeal*, November 16, 1995.

Memphis Heritage. "Normal Station." Accessed June 9, 2014. http://www.memphisheritage.org/normal-station.

"Negroes Served by Tea Room." *Memphis Press-Scimitar*, October 3, 1986.

Ogle, Jimmy. Email to Caitlin L. Horton. September 8, 2014.

"Sit in Staged at Tea Room." *Memphis Press-Scimitar*, October 3, 1986.

"Trying for Truce in Café Picketing." *Memphis Press-Scimitar*, May 8, 1964.

CHAPTER THIRTEEN

Berkhalter, Denise. "Old, Young Populate and Protect 'Leahyville.'" *The Commercial Appeal*, July 29, 1995.

Jensen, George and JoAnne Jensen. Interview by Caitlin L. Horton. June 9, 2014.

Lauderdale, Vance. "Life at Leahy's." Accessed February 10, 2013. http://www.memphismagazine.com/Memphis-Magazine/September-2010/Life-at-Leahy-039s.

Musselwhite, Charlie. Interview by Caitlin L. Horton. August 14, 2014.

Musselwhite, Charlie. Liner notes to *One Night in America*. Charlie Musselwhite. Telarc. CD. 2002.

Page, Betty. *I Got Ya Elvis, I Got Ya!* Memphis: Pages' Publishing, 1977.

Page, Betty. Interview by Caitlin L. Horton and Rebecca Phillips. June 25, 2013.

Prewitt, Ellen Morris. "Summer Avenue." Accessed July 6, 2013. http://www.storysouth.com/nonfiction/2007/02/summer_avenue.html.

Scott, Anna. Interview by Rebecca Phillips and Caitlin L. Horton. June 25, June 27, 2013.

Sonsky, Lindsay. "From Beverly Hills to a Trailer Park on Summer." *East Memphis Appeal*, February 20, 2005.

CHAPTER FOURTEEN

Davenport, Jimmy. E-mail to Rebecca Phillips. April 3, 2014.

Dunn, Darla. Interview by Rebecca Phillips. May 13, 2014.

"Family Cabana Swim Club Planned." *Memphis Press Scimitar*, April 18, 1958.

Flickr. "Southern Regional Skate Championship" *Birch from Memphis*. Accessed June 9, 2014. https://www.flickr.com/photos/51992558@N00/8979592883.

Hall, Trisha. Interview by Rebecca Phillips. May 13, 2014.

Johnson, Yolanda. "Fire Chars Skateland." *The Commercial Appeal*, January 21, 2006.

Lauderdale, Vance. "Skateland on Summer." Ask Vance blog. July 19, 2009. http://www.memphisflyer.com/AskVanceBlog/archives/2009/07/19/skateland-on-summer.

Moyes, David. Interview by Rebecca Phillips. May 13, 2014.

Roadside Architecture. "Skating Signs." Accessed June 9, 2014. http://agilitynut.com/sca/skating.html.

Russell, Ron. "Memphis Roller Skating." *The Commercial Appeal*, January 25, 1987.

Skateland. "Roller Skating History of the United States." Skateland website. Accessed June 9, 2014. http://skateland.com/rshis.html.

Strain, Hartwell. Interview by Rebecca Phillips. March 28, 2014.

Sweazy, Caleb. Interview by Rebecca Phillips. March 27, 2014.

Sweazy, Melissa. "Firebrand Furniture." Thoroughly Modern Medusa Head blog. September 12, 2008. http://www.modernmedusahead.com/2008/09/firebrand-furniture.html.

CHAPTER FIFTEEN

Andrews, Barbara. Interview by Caitlin L. Horton. May 29, 2014.

Civil Rights Museum. "Freedom Awards." Accessed June 8, 2014. http://civilrightsmuseum.org/freedom-awards.

"Eviction Empties Motel Where Dr. King Died." *The New York Times*, March 3, 1988. http://www.nytimes.com/1988/03/03/us/eviction-empties-motel-where-dr-king-died.html.

Jones, John Paul, III. "The Street Politics of Jackie Smith." *The Blackwell Companion to the City*, eds. Gary Bridge and Sophie Watson. Oxford: Blackwell, 2011.

Preston, Lauterbach. "The Crucible." *Memphis Magazine*, April 2008. http://www.memphismagazine.com/April-2008/The-Crucible.

Qualy, Erica. Interview by Rebecca Phillips. March 8, 2014.

CHAPTER SIXTEEN

Buskin, Richard. "Sam Phillips: Sun Records." Sound on Sound website. Accessed June 8, 2014. http://www.soundonsound.com/sos/oct03/articles/samphillips.htm.

Dawson, Walter. "Presley and Phillips Had Nothing to Lose by Being Different." *The Commercial Appeal*, August 1, 1978.

Jensen, Carolyn. Interview by Caitlin L. Horton. May 22, 2014.

Jones, Memphis. Interview by Rebecca Phillips. March 24, 2014.

Moore, Scotty. "Sam Phillips Recording Service." Scotty Moore, Official Website. Accessed June 8, 2014. http://scottymoore.net/studio_phillips.html.

Rosebrough, Richard. E-mail to Rebecca Phillips. May 17, 2014.

Roy, James. E-mail to Rebecca Phillips. May 13, 2014.

"Sam Phillips." *Biography*. Accessed June 8, 2014. http://www.biography.com/people/ sam-phillips-20943313#awesm=~oEZdH4BkU4xukB.

Sanderson, Jane. "Restoration of the Sun Records Studio is Nearing Completion." *The Commercial Appeal*, November 7, 1978.

Shultz, Barbara. "Sam Phillips." Mix Professional Audio and Music Production website. October 1, 2000. http://mixonline.com/mag/audio_sam_phillips.

CHAPTER SEVENTEEN

706 Union Avenue Sessions. "Memphis from 1000 through 1928." Accessed June 9, 2014. http:// www.706unionavenue.nl/68811865.

B.B. King. "King Biography." B.B. King website. Accessed June 9, 2014. http://www.bbking.com/bio.

Cheseborough, Steve. *Blues Traveling: The Holy Sites of Delta Blues*, Third Edition. Jackson, MS: University Press of Mississippi, 2009.

Jones, Memphis. Interview by Rebecca Phillips. March 24, 2014.

Notable Names Database. "B. B. King." NNDB.com. Accessed June 9, 2014. http://www.nndb.com/ people/136/000023067.

Peters, Thomas. Interview by Caitlin L. Horton. June 2, 2014.

WDIA AM1070. "Celebrating 65 Years of Goodwill & Good Times." WDIA AM1070 website. Accessed June 9, 2014. http://www.mywdia.com/pages/history/about/#ixzz34CD9Uwpdhttp://www.mywdia .com/pages/history/about.

Wright, Sarah. Interview by Caitlin L. Horton and Rebecca Phillips. June 9, 2014.

CHAPTER EIGHTEEN

Alley, Richard J. "Soulful Synergy." *Memphis Daily News*, December 7, 2013. Accessed May 22, 2014. http://www.memphisdailynews.com/news/2013/dec/7/soulful-synergy.

Bates, Willie. Interview by Caitlin L. Horton. May 2014.

Blank, Christopher. "Reprising Role as Racial Respite." *The Commerical Appeal*, April 30, 2003.

Myers, Marc. "Stax's Legacy is Reborn After School." *The Wall Street Journal*, August 31, 2011. Accessed May 21, 2014. http://online.wsj.com/news/articles/SB10001424053111903596904576514141964564846.

Ogle, Jimmy. Interview by Caitlin L. Horton. May 2014.

Perkins, Pamela. "Stax Museum Group Adapts 'Soulsville' as New Name, Attitude." *The Commerical Appeal*, October 19, 2000.

Russell, Maggie. Interview by Caitlin L. Horton. May 2014.

Sampson, Tim. E-mail to Caitlin L. Horton. June 6, 2014.

Sampson, Tim. "Rightly Seasoned." *Memphis Magazine*, March 2014. Accessed May 20, 2014. http://www.memphismagazine.com/March-2014/Rightly-Seasoned.

Sampson, Tim. "The Rant." *Memphis Flyer*, May 31, 2012. Accessed May 23, 2014. http://www.memphisflyer.com/memphis/the-rant/Content?oid=3195624.

Saries, Bob. *Soulsville*. Documentary film. 2003. STAX Museum of American Soul Music.

"Soul Music 101: Taking a Walk Through the History of Stax Records." *Chicago Sun-Times*, February 1, 2004.

Soulsville Foundation. "About." Accessed May 20, 2014. http://www.soulsvillefoundation.org/#about.

Stax Museum of American Soul Music. "History." Accessed May 20, 2014. http://www.staxmuseum.com/about/history.

Weiler, Joseph. "Stax Records: The Dream That Died." *The Commercial Appeal*, February 9, 1976.

CHAPTER NINETEEN

Bailey, Stoy. Interview by Caitlin L. Horton. May 15, 2014.

Bailey, Thomas, Jr. "New Restaurant Proclaims 'Midtown Is Memphis.'" *The Commercial Appeal*, March 8, 2013. http://www.commercialappeal.com/news/2013/mar/08/new-restaurant-proclaims-midtown-is-memphis/?CID= happeningnow.

Bailey, Tom, Jr. "Overton Square Project Retooled." *The Commercial Appeal*, August 31, 2011.

Baker, Sarah. "Work Moves Forward on Midtown's Chiwawa." *Memphis Daily News* 127, no. 169. August 29, 2012.

Berger, Taylor. Interview by Rebecca Phillips. February 18, 2014.

Darnell, David. "It Tolls For Overton Square." *The Commercial Appeal*, November 9, 1970.

Darnell, Dan. "Overton Square - The Early Years." Photograph no. 32. *The Commercial Appeal*. Accessed June 8, 2014. http://www.commercialappeal.com/photos/galleries/overton-square---early-years/41735.

"Demolition Request Filed for Square." *The Commercial Appeal*, December 12, 2009.

Finger, Michael. "When It Was Hip To Be Square." *Memphis Magazine*, January 2008. Accessed June 8, 2014. http://www.memphismagazine.com/January-2008/When-It-Was-Hip-To-Be-Square.

Gardner, Richard. "Overton Square - The Early Years." Photograph no. 20, *The Commercial Appeal*, Accessed June 8, 2014. http://www.commercialappeal.com/photos/galleries/overton-square---early-years/41724.

Hattiloo. "Hattiloo Theater." Hattiloo.org. Accessed May 4, 2014. http://hattiloo.org/hattiloo.php.

Levenstein, Steve. "Good Pie & Farewell: 10 Crusty Old Abandoned Pizzerias." Web Urbanist website. Accessed June 8, 2014. http://weburbanist.com/2013/08/18/good-pie-farewell-10-crusty-old-abandoned-pizzerias/3.

"New Shop Plans, Hotel Interests, Trail Drink OK." *The Commercial Appeal*, November 27, 1969.

O'Shaughnessy, Lynn. "Residential Mainstay in Overton Square: Little Cottage Across from Fridays." *Memphis Press Scimitar*, June 19, 1979.

Pendergrass, Dianne. Interview by Caitlin L. Horton. February 24, 2014.

Risher, Wayne "Overton Square Battles Image." *The Commercial Appeal*, September 13, 1993.

Sankey, Bruce. "Overton Square Expansion." *The Commercial Appeal*, April 13, 1975.

West, June. Interview by Rebecca Phillips. April 29, 2014.

Whooten, Drew. Interview by Rebecca Phillips. February 18, 2014.

About

THE AUTHOR

Caitlin L. Horton received a BA in International Studies and French and an MA in French at the University of Mississippi. Like the blues, she came from the Delta to make a home in Memphis. She and her husband will continue to explore the ins and outs of this uniquely gritty and endlessly interesting city.

THE ARTIST

Rebecca Phillips received a BFA in Communication Design at Texas State University, San Marcos. Although she was born and raised in Texas, Phillips calls Memphis home after moving in 2008. She currently lives in the Midtown area as a mother, wife, and painter.

Read more at
memphistypehistory.com

CPSIA information can be obtained
at www.ICGtesting.com
Printed in the USA
LVHW011106041019
633145LV00003B/3/P

9 780692 308059